# THE CONSULTATIVE RECRUITER

## YOUR REAL KEY TO

Fill Reqs Faster
Attract Great Candidates
Have More Influence with
Your Hiring Managers

## Katherine moody

LEGAL NOTICE (the blah, blah, blah omitted):

Please use this information in any way that will help you.

**Updated Bonus Reports:**
The link to all updates, ebook version of this report is on page *Consultative Recruiting Forms, Templates & Reports* at the end of this book .

You will find all the special forms in the zip file. I wanted you to have them as word docs so you can modify them to fit your situations (and hiring managers!).

Contact me if you have a hiring manager challenge or any recruiting situation you'd like to brainstorm. We'll come up with a new approach that will make all the difference. You'll love the results!

If you would like to talk about training and team and/or individual coaching, please let me know.

**Katherine@ConsultativeRecruiting.com**

**832.464.4447**

**Schedule a complimentary consulting call here:** https://meetme.so/AllAboutYou

Wishing you great success and epic recruiting results as you implement these techniques and concepts.

Best of luck to you, my consultative recruiter friend,

*Katherine*

P. S. Be sure to watch the video    https://screencast-o-matic.com/u/jUa0/

# Contents

# 2020 Update: What's New

**Real Life Stories**: I've added lots of these so you can read how other recruiters used the techniques and strategies to solve real life issues. I hope they will serve as guidelines to using the techniques to get great results.

The stories are indented and in italics so you can find them easily. I don't know about you, but I often go through books looking for stories and examples to read first. If you do that, too, go for it!

New Sections: (On the ebook version, just jlick on the page number in the Table of Contents to zip off to read the new sections.)

## What you and your hiring managers have in common

### Today's recruiting realities:

- Goldfish Theory (the fish not the cracker) changes all the old communication rules
- The recruiting iceberg
- A deadly misunderstanding: The promise AI tools can never keep
- The most important factor for recruiting success

### Good intentions that backfire on recruiters

- A French Fry moment: shattering the order taker stereotype
- How to lose credibility while trying to please them
- Why under promising and over delivering wipes out your credibility
- Why over under promising and over delivering totally wipes out your credibility

## 5 Principals of Consultative Recruiting

## 5 Ways to Build and Reinforce Your Consultative Recruiter Image

## Updated Bonus Reports:

See Now It's Your Turn to get the link to all the updates, ebook version of this book.

# Recruiter as Trusted Advisor: Case Study

*EB, Talent Acquisition, Media Technology*

Search status when training began:

- 4 similar positions open for at least 2 months with no offers extended
- Had received and reviewed over 150 resumes
- Screened several people, presented 3 and all were rejected by the hiring manager
- Candidate response was declining
- Hiring manager expressing concern about filling the positions
- Hiring process was long and presented significant scheduling challenges
- Interview process included 2-3 panel interviews to accommodate the 6 peers of the position who wanted to be included in the decision, all of whom seemed to have different definitions of the role requirements

Actions taken by the recruiter:

- Removed the job description posting
- Scheduled a launch meeting with the hiring manager and the 6 peers
- Used the tools and techniques from Recruiter as Trusted Advisor training to prepare for and conduct the first-time-ever launch meeting

Outcome:

- Hiring manager realized the original job description was no longer accurate, and a new definition of the position, requirements, etc., was defined
- The 6 peers were now in agreement about the requirements and definition of success for the role
- A new posting was created using the information from the launch meeting
- The old phone screen was replaced with a more relevant (and shorter) screen based on the launch meeting information
- Peers changed their questions for the panel interviews to accurately reflect what they were looking for

Results:

- Within 6 weeks of the launch meeting, 3 positions had been filled, with an offer for the 4th about to be made
- Fewer resumes were received from the new posting, with a significantly higher percentage of them qualified for the position, reducing the time the recruiter had to spend reviewing resumes
- Recruiter spent significantly less time in each screening call because most of the questions about the position she previously had to answer are already answered via the posting

Impact on hiring manager-recruiter relationship:

- Hiring manager has included the recruiter in more discussions about the position, candidates, and the future of the role to do some workforce planning (a first!)
- Hiring manager provides more feedback about candidates and provides it sooner after an interview

- Hiring manager and recruiter are collaborating for the first time on the process, next steps for each candidate, etc., for this and additional requisitions

Recap:

- Initial Status: 4 positions and absolutely no hires in 2 months
- Recruiter conducted an hour meeting with the hiring manager using the tools and techniques from the training
- Recruiter rewrote the posting and the recruiter screening questions
- Within the next 6 weeks, she got 3 fills and 4<sup>th</sup> offer about to be made

UPDATE: That 4<sup>th</sup> offer was accepted!

# What Other Recruiters Want You to Know

"This training has changed everything—for the better. **Before the training, we had never hit our monthly hiring targets. After the training, we are now hitting them month after month.** The hiring managers have used the term "life changing"."

**VP, Talent Acquisition, Hospitality Industry**

"I have to tell you- that was the best intake meeting I have ever had. The **hiring manager said she was thoroughly impressed with the process,** the level of detail I was digging into, and that this was the most in-depth discussion she had had to date about a position when hiring for it. From this particular manager, especially, this was a huge compliment. So thank you! Your insight and guidance has been amazing."

**HB., Senior Recruiter, Media Technology**

"Typically I wouldn't have had the courage to {have a conversation} with this VP. It felt empowering to be able to have that conversation and I didn't leave the meeting thinking there was something I wasn't doing. I used to beat myself up because I couldn't have those discussions, but not now! **These are small changes you can implement right away and see big impact right away.**"

*DM., Talent Acquisition, Retail*

"The time I have spent with Katherine has given me the tools needed to become a Trusted Advisor. Utilizing the skills I have developed working with Katherine; I am focused on creating a meaningful, productive partnership with the Hiring Manager and sourcing candidates to meet their needs. I am **no longer taking orders**, but instead anticipating the wants and needs of the Hiring Manager and providing a great candidate experience. Through her guidance and training, I am able to **save countless hours** every week. Katherine provided me the tools needed to have **meaningful conversations with Hiring Managers and candidates** which allowed me to **fill positions quicker.** Katherine is a world-class talent acquisition mentor and coach!"

*HB., Senior Corporate Recruiter, Technology*

"It was good to hear about how the words you choose can change relationships, and how to pick words so people don't take offense but can hear what you are saying. **This is the first time I ever heard anything like this.**"

*AP, Senior Corporate Recruiter, Consumer Marketing*

I went into it doubting I would learn anything because I've been recruiting for a long time. This was **refreshing and interesting.** Well presented. Good solid examples and topics. I am very impressed."

*MD, Contract Recruiter, Entertainment Technology*

I wasn't sure what I would get out of this, but it was definitely worth it. I had never had such a clear explanation of the simple word choices that can make a difference in being seen as credible. My biggest "aha" was in the discussion around having conversations that allow me to have more influence and credibility (as Katherine promised). That resulted in them agreeing to make the change I wanted in the first place!"

*TP, Senior Corporate Recruiter, Media*

"The ideas on how to effectively communicate and **redirect some of the behavior we experience with non-engaged hiring managers was exactly what we needed in our current high-pressure environment**. It also helped us with isolating some of the issues we have due to our lack of capacity to manage relationships in a most effective manner with our hiring managers."

*VP, Recruiter, Finance*

"Katherine Moody trained my Talent Acquisition team on the Trusted Advisor training and coaching sessions which helped transform my team from "order takers" to valued consultants. Katherine shared tools as well as best practices that made this transition quick and seamless. I have received numerous compliments from Hiring Managers in addition to **reducing time to fill** from 70-80 days to 40-50 days for most vacancies."

*AC., TA Manager, Technology*

"Instead of 6 calls to the hiring manager, it took just one simply change that has improved my relationships in a matter of weeks. I think about my relationships before. I had relationships with hiring managers for over 2 years, and I didn't get the same relationship that I do now in a matter of weeks.

I also had success with rewriting a posting for a position here in Denver. As usual the hiring manager loved the new approach. She interviewed with two strong internal and two strong external candidates. True to form, **we see less candidates but the right candidates. This reduces everyone's time in the screening process.** "

**PM,** *Talent Acquisition, Broadband Technology*

"The things I learned in the consultative recruiter training made it possible for me to get a promotion to a recruiter position from a recruiting coordinator role."

**EG,** *Excited New Corporate Recruiter*

# Two Success Examples That Have Nothing to do with Recruiting

## The Homework Struggle is Over

Tim is a TA Director who attended my live Consultative Recruiter master class and used the techniques in the book consistently and successfully. His relationship with his most difficult hiring manager had been improved significantly.

The hiring manager who used to complain about him was now telling the VP Talent how happy he was with Tim's performance.

One day, Tim asked if I thought he could use some of the strategies with his 10-year old son. He was struggling to get his son to do homework, and nothing he was trying seemed to make a difference. Great idea!

Here is what Tim told me:

*"One night when my son was refusing to do his homework, rather than ask my typical "why" questions and do what I've always done, I used some of the Consultative Recruiter strategies. For the first time, I understood the reason for what was going on with him. He and I came up with some ideas to help him. For the first time in a long time, he went to do his homework without our typical arguments.*

*And you know what? That has been the case for every night since. Our house is more peaceful thanks to your techniques. Thank you from our whole family."*

## The Trash Goes Out Willingly

*"I started using these techniques, especially the questions guidelines, at home. I'm not sure which technique it was, but for the first time in ages, my husband took out the trash without me having to ask! I cannot wait to see what else happens but if this is the only change, I'm still a happy camper."*

*TC, Talent Acquisition Associate, Hospitality*

# The Fastest Way to Get the Most Benefit

You'll be able to put each technique here into action right away. And you'll see results the very first time you try each one.

But you don't have to put *all* of them into action right away. And you absolutely must not wait until you think you can do it perfectly!

Go to the **Quick Start Checklist** in the back and pick one situation you've been experiencing. Read the techniques that will help you resolve and transform it. Do them. Repeat, etc.

I used to read a book, get lots of ideas and get all excited to start seeing a difference somewhere in my life or career. Then I closed the book, put it on a shelf (ideally where I couldn't see it), or some place on my computer (that of course I could never remember) and never did any of the things recommended. I think that's what most of us do, so if you have done that before, you're in good company.

For some reason, I thought in order to get results, I would have to put everything into action all at once and right away. And that was just too overwhelming for me. So usually I would end up doing nothing!

What I am delighted to share with you is the best way to get benefit from these techniques--just start with one. That's the way to make real progress—one at a time, one after another.

What you'll find here is exactly what you need to know to become as good at consultative recruiting as you want.

## 4 Simple Steps to Ensure Your Success

1. **Look for the twist that makes the technique really effective**
   When we see easy common-sense approaches to things, it can look obvious—and you may find yourself think-ing, "Well, I already knew that. So what?"

   Try to avoid that. The real thing often looks obvious. So please don't think that you can skip the technique because you already know it. Before you skip it, look for the subtlety that I've added to these techniques. I was able to add the little twists that will make these so very effective for you.

2. **Just try to do one technique every day**
   Don't try to implement all of these or even a large portion of them overnight. You can be considerably better in a week if you will just aim for a little improvement every day. And each improvement actually builds on everything you've done to date, so you'll be amazed at how quickly you see fabulous results with just a little effort.

   It may be a little difficult at first to see how such small improvements are ever going to add up to a big difference, but they will. Every technique is a proven strategy that will work in your real world. So no matter where you start with these techniques, you'll see improvement.

3. **Apply the material in each lesson immediately**

   If you want to see real results, be sure to use the technique you've read as soon as possible. Remember just pick one technique or two. Then use it, see results, modify as necessary. Lather, rinse, repeat.

   I know it's so easy to get caught up in all the other aspects of your recruiting req load that you forget or decide to forgo for today using what you're learning. At some point you will regret that.

   It's not easy but essential to just stop and decide you're going to use just one of these techniques.

4. **Review the techniques**

   After you've used a technique a few times, go back and read the explanation one more time. You may find additional finesse that you can add to your implementation so you get even better results.

# Introduction: Long Ago and Far Away

The real beginning of my attempt to craft a psychology for creating true business partner relationships was nearly 20 years ago. I was a director of marketing for a national software development firm. Our CEO had just gotten a new, very large and very important client to mandate all of their U.S. offices use our product—an industry first--for us and for our client.

The lead partner at our new client insisted that the CEO designate someone in our company to serve as the liaison between their offices and our individual processing centers around the country. This was certainly one of those positions no one in their right mind would take—it was fraught with political landmines on both sides.

But with my lethal mixture of naiveté, inexperience and rampant excitement, I agree to take on the position in addition to my other job duties. And that was the beginning of my focused study on how to quickly create credible business relationships and be seen as a Trusted Advisor with people who were far senior to me, had little time for me, and, at first, had absolutely no vested interest in my success or even making my life easier.

I was really scared about how to do this. But it was clear I had to create strong, credible relationships with people who really didn't want to be doing business with us and initially saw me merely as a person who was supposed to make life easier for them.

Making life easier for them certainly was my goal, but I didn't want to be viewed as just another vendor. I wanted a much stronger, more professional and potentially lasting relationship with them. And by gosh I was going to create that—even if they didn't initially want to play.

The next five months were absolutely the most difficult of my career to that point. But this was the best training ground I could have had to develop and practice the psychology of creating credible business relationships and becoming a Trusted Advisor. Of course, I wouldn't want you to think it just took those five months and yippee! Everyone respected me.

Nope. But I did start to develop the concepts that are at the core of all the things I will share in these techniques.

**And one more time…**

Nearly 10 years later, after a career change, there I was, scared to death again because I had landed a job as Director of Experienced Hiring for the Western Tax Region of Deloitte & Touche. I had really wanted that job. There I was again with that lethal mixture of naiveté, inexperience and rampant enthusiasm.

However, I landed that role even though I only had about 3 months of recruiting experience at a small boutique firm in Newport Beach.

I had a Director title, but that didn't mean I had any one to direct. I was the department. I stopped counting the open requisitions when I reached 250. Plus I had 20+ hiring managers, all of whom, you guessed it, coincidentally had critical positions that had to be filled right away.

Even though there was a lot of work to do, I took some time to prioritize what really needed to happen at some point and what needed to happen *right away*. I decided to get some quick wins so I could catch my breath and figure out how I was going to do this.

At the very beginning, I did a few very visible things that quickly improved the process time. Since they had neither processes nor technology in place, that was pretty easy to do. Of course I didn't tell them just how easy those things were to accomplish.

I knew I also had to quickly create relationships with the hiring managers. They were resource constrained (which in that environment mean they were not able to sell as much business as they wanted because they simply did not have enough people to provide the services they sold). So that translated to really nice people being really frustrated.

As they saw it, recruiting (meaning ME) was preventing them for doing a great job and even worse, severely impacting their income in a very negative way.

At this point, I thought all I had to do was find them great candidates to hire, and we would have good working relationships. It was a major shock when I realized a) finding great candidates was simply not enough and b) without great relationships with my hiring managers, I was never going to be really successful.

As a result of a lot of my trying new things, discarding what wasn't working, and continuing to refine and retry what did seem to work, I came up with these techniques.

When you start to use them, you will build stronger, more credible business relationships with your hiring managers than you ever thought possible and build your reputation as a Trusted Advisor.

I hope you'll try them. I think you'll love the results.

# Recruiters and Hiring Managers: Like Ships Passing in the Night?

In almost all of our consulting and recruiting assignments we hear recruiters say, "The hiring managers should… (Fill in the blank with probably the same things you say)".

We usually cannot argue with that statement, regardless of how they (and you) fill in that blank--it's true. Traditionally, we as recruiters are not specifically taught how to create effective working partnerships with our hiring managers.

There may be a "process" meeting, and everyone agrees how to move forward. Everyone seems to be on the same team with the same goals. My experience is that arrangement is short lived. Have you been disappointed, as so many others have, because things pretty quickly go back to the "old normal"?

So you may find yourself in a recruiting environment where everyone seems to accept an underlying reality wherein the recruiter just has to live with what the hiring managers are doing. The unspoken rule seems to be that recruiters just have to make everything work.

Sometimes recruiters think that if they just work hard enough, find lots of great candidates, are accommodating often enough, they will have proven themselves. If that were all it took to create great business partner relationships, most recruiters I know would have those relationships right now.

I believe recruiters should be viewed as the experts in their field because, after all, you are! I also believe recruiters and hiring managers should be in the recruiting game together, and each take responsibility for their respective portions.

And when you use the strategies in this book, you will start to see that happen. But it won't happen automatically, it won't happen if we give recruiters new titles like "talent advisor", and it won't happen if we as recruiters just wait for hiring managers to understand the value add we bring.

We also often hear hiring managers say, "Recruiting is the job of the recruiter. Recruiting isn't my job."

I don't know any recruiters who agree with that philosophy. It's not rocket science that recruiting works best when everyone in the company understands they play a critical role in the success of recruiting.

**So what's a recruiter to do?**

There is actually a lot you can do to create the kind of environment where everyone really understands the role they play and the importance of that role. With these techniques, you can start to get the kinds of changes you have been asking for.

---

*It just takes one person willing to make changes to change the relationship.*

---

We all certainly have a lot of experience with a relationship going bad because of the actions of one of the people in that relationship. Well, the opposite is possible as well.

I believe the one with the flexibility wins. If you are willing to be flexible, try some simple yet powerful techniques, you will have an improved and more useful relationship with your hiring managers.

You cannot "mandate" that people cooperate with you, take responsibility for something or become accountable. If you wait for them to "get it" it may be a long wait. However, you absolutely can accelerate their "getting it" by using the techniques you'll learn here.

Maybe you've seen your hiring manager treat an external recruiter from a search firm the way you want to be treated. Now you'll learn here what that external recruiter does. There are the techniques I learned while working with a very smart partner at Heidrick and Struggles. I'll share his secrets.

It's all in the way the recruiter deals with the hiring manager. It's in the way the recruiter thinks of themselves in relation to the hiring manager. It's a relationship of equals—both acknowledging the professional expertise of the other. Then you will be seen as a trusted advisor.

In some companies, I've noticed recruiters think they don't have the education, the business acumen, the expertise, etc., etc., to consider themselves an equal to an executive hiring manager. You can still be respectful in your dealings with the hiring manager. I'm just encouraging you to step into your professional role as an equal who is the expert.

# What You and Your Hiring Managers have in Common

As you read this, please know that I do not intend to bash hiring managers nor make light of all they have on their plates. In fact, it's interesting to see how much you and the hiring manager actually have in common. Just a few of those things are:

| Hiring Managers | You and Your Recruiters |
|---|---|
| Well intentioned and committed to doing a good job | Well intentioned and committed to doing a good job |
| Busy doing lots of things in their job on which they are evaluated | Busy doing lots of things in your job on which you are evaluated |
| Wear many hats while managing their function, department or business with multiple "customers" | Wear many hats with internal and external "customers" |
| Often not able to focus on filling positions that would make their life easier | Often not able to focus on doing some of the things that would make recruiting easier |
| Sometimes and at some level may believe "recruiting is not their job" without realizing how negatively that impacts your recruiting results | Know "recruiting is your job" but also know that hiring managers have huge impact on your success |
| Sometimes not eager to change | Sometimes not eager to change |

With the following techniques, you'll learn how to claim your rightful position as their consultative recruiter--how to avoid blowing that image, and how to expand that image in every interaction with your hiring managers.

# 5 Principals of Consultative Recruiting

Consultative Recruiter Principals

Lead by asking more questions

Ask and be silent

Small questions they can answer

Be curious about what they are thinking

Don't leave without details

Good news!

You just need 5 key principals to build stronger partnerships with your hiring managers, while filling positions faster and landing more great candidates. If you follow these 5 principals consistently, use as many of them in each situation as you need, and believe in your skill and expertise, you're going to love the results.

In the stories of what other recruiters have done, you will see that each story often combines several principals at the same time.

You'll see that they really aren't separate.

With this simple foundation, you'll be able to successfully manage all your recruiting challenges, whether with candidates, hiring managers, your boss, etc.

# 5 Ways to Build & Reinforce Your Consultative Recruiter Image

## Make small promises—keep them.

When was the last time someone did what they said they would do—when they said they would do it? As an aside, I once asked a sales exec who had become a millionaire selling office cleaning supplies what was his secret to success. This simple strategy was what had made him a trusted business partner to his customers. Think how it can add to your business relationships to be known as someone who delivers on their commitments.

## Be willing to talk about the elephant.

It may be difficult but when you say what has to be said, you create a tremendous amount of trust. Ask the critical question that everyone is thinking. Sometimes saying the thing that is most difficult to say is the thing that will build the most trust. Just don't throw anyone under the bus, of course.

## Let your passion and excitement show.

HM's like it when you are excited (honestly) about recruiting for their position. When you can generate genuine excitement, it will also help you write a powerful posting and an LinkIn inmail your target candidates will take the time to open.

## Confidence generates confidence.

The "fake it until you make it" approach never worked for me. I found it difficult to come across as confident when I'm feeling like a fake—maybe it's just me. So to create genuine confidence, remember: YOU are the recruiting expert. I know everyone in the company may think they can do your job, but you and I know they could not. So trust yourself and your skills, share your knowledge and perspective and know that you know what you're doing.

## Simple phrases for consultants.

- "Does that make sense?"
- "What are your thoughts about..."
- "Would that work for you?"
- "Would you tell me more about your thoughts on...?"
- "I was mistaken."

In the next section, we'll talk about some of today's recruiting realities. The recruiting environment has always been multi-faceted. But there are several new realities that can impact your job satisfaction and performance big time! Here are three of the newest and how to leverage them without being blindsided by them.

# Today's Recruiting Realities

## *Goldfish theory (the fish not the cracker) changes all the old rules of communication*

Here is some weird and essential information about what really makes all the difference in how we communicate to build credibility and trusting relationships in the world today.

### Are You Paying Attention?

Recent research from Harvard University reveals this startling finding that reflects how today's technology is impacting all of us. And it may not be what you expect.

The research concluded that most adults today have an attention span of about 7 seconds. Think about how quickly you tune people out if they are talking on and on, how likely you are to click to move to the next thing on the internet, watch two movies or sports events at the same time, and slide to the next screen on your phone and table. And how strange is this—we often feel guilty if we aren't multi-tasking!

I wonder if we even pay attention for seven seconds anymore; this research was done about 4 years ago.

And what else did they find in the research? (Wish I'd been there to watch this!) Turns out a goldfish will pay attention to something about nine seconds before they think it's boring. What does this mean?

It means that the changes that you're experiencing in terms of how information needs to be presented, how long you will pay attention, and how little attention you may be paying is also true for your hiring managers. Actually it's true for your peers, the people in HR with whom you interact, your boss, your candidates and probably everyone else you know.

So now there is no way to deny those changes have happened to all of us. What it also means you must change how you communicate. I'm going to share that with you because that's a big part of what the consultative recruiter's all about.

When you change how you communicate, you are leveraging the fact that people have a short attention span. The more you acknowledge this new reality, the more effective your communication will be.

To make sure your communication has any impact these days, in our world where we are all on information overload, it must be concise, relevant and memorable. The best way to connect with people who have shorter and shorter attention spans, is to use techniques like:

- metaphors,
- stories and examples,
- bottom-line conclusions,
- asking questions rather than making statements,
- constructing images that represent the point you want them to get, etc.

***Tough love for all of us***: if your conversation sounds like a lecture, goes on and on with no end in sight, or your hiring managers think they have heard it all before, they will simply move on--at least mentally. You have lost their attention. They may be looking at you, but they are thinking about lunch!

Of course, what you have to say is important. It is equally important to start changing HOW you say it. That is a key success factor in building your consultative recruiter status with strong hiring manager business partnerships.

And that is exactly what I will show you how to do.

## *The Recruiting Iceberg*

The second reality I have identified around recruiting is that most people in your company know very little about what you really do or the multiple challenges you have while doing it!

Regardless, they often are convinced they know all about recruiting. They may even be thinking they know more about it than you do. And sometimes, it feels like they even think they could do it better than you.

Many people in the company often think recruiting is just about sourcing candidates. And then they think, "Well, how hard can that be? We have LinkedIn, we post jobs, we have resume sourcing services. So candidates just show up, right?"

Maybe they also know you do things like post the job, screen the candidates, follow up after interviews, etc. That is probably what they experienced when they were hired. But every non-recruiter has a very limited perspective of what recruiting really does.

Here is a simple illustration of what is invisible to most people in your company:

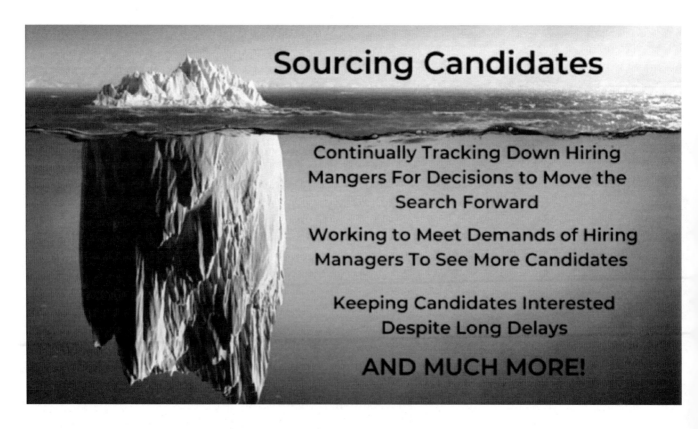

**Sourcing Candidates**

Continually Tracking Down Hiring Mangers For Decisions to Move the Search Forward

Working to Meet Demands of Hiring Managers To See More Candidates

Keeping Candidates Interested Despite Long Delays

AND MUCH MORE!

This is because the things that really impact the speed of filling the req are below the water line of the iceberg. Interestingly, these are some of the things that also influence how happy your manager and your hiring managers are with your performance.

---

*The things that have the greatest impact
on the speed of getting reqs filled are usually
invisible to everyone else.*

---

So you're filling reqs but time-to-fill stats are waaay too long. Perhaps you sense your manager and/or the hiring managers don't seem to be happy. It's almost always because the things that really demand your time and expertise are invisible to them.

Of course, the catch-22 is you cannot simply list off these things to your hiring managers. First, it can sound like a lecture. Second, I've been surprised to learn that hiring managers **hear** that as making excuses.

Neither is your intention, but that is today's communication reality. So if it won't work to just tell people all the value-add things you do as a recruiter, are you doomed to them never understanding and you being under-appreciated?

Absolutely not! Check out the **Technique 2 Questions: The Secret to Taking Control**

## A Deadly Misunderstanding: A Promise Artificial Intelligence Tools Can Never Keep

I wanted to share this often-overlooked and ever-increasing reality with you because I think it does represent a potential landmine for us as recruiters. At the same time, we can leverage this reality to continue to build a consultative recruiter relationship.

Most AI tools including your ATS, pre-screening questions on line, testing questions candidates have to answer as part of the on-line application process, as well as today's resume-finding services, promise more candidates faster, all with less recruiter effort.

This reality is about **the gap**. This is the gap between hiring manager expectations that recruiting is now going to be faster with a lot of perfect candidates and the reality that artificial intelligence tools will never be able to fulfill those expectations.

First, as you probably realize, the promises of AI tools are based on that same misconception about what recruiting really is. Hiring Managers start to believe that because your new AI tools will produce lots of candidates quickly, recruiting issues are totally eliminated. This is the result of believing recruiting is just about getting lots o'candidates.

How does this gap get created?

Two main reasons:

1. The belief that recruiting is just a linear process and all that **needs to happen,** is you as recruiter get lots of people to the door, and then one of those people falls into the chair. It's just a straight line. How hard can it be?

2. So because AI tools promise lots of great candidates very fast, recruiting will be improved—hiring problems solved.

Of course, the "more candidates" promise doesn't necessarily mean a faster and easier hiring process for hiring managers.

If they continue to do the things that can prolong the time it takes to fill the position, more candidates won't solve that issue. So the result will be a gap between what hiring managers are expecting and the reality of what those tools really mean for the hiring process.

The Hiring Manager can also concludes that they don't have to do anything differently; all hiring issues and challenges are now solved with these new tools.

As we saw with the recruiting iceberg, most people don't understand all of the things that have to happen between the door and that previously vacant chair.

So what happens when those expectations aren't met? It's understandable that those hiring managers may conclude it has to do with your efforts as their recruiter

You can actually use that gap to become a consultative recruiter when you:

a) recognize what your hiring managers may be expecting from the implementation of your AI tools, and

b) you use the strategies and techniques in this book to bridge the gap.

I'm going to show you exactly how to do that! It's easier and much more fun than you might think

## The Most Important Factor for Recruiting Success

Recruiters have an interesting challenge in the corporate environment because they have both external and internal customers. Recruiters almost always enjoy the external facing part of their job. They love the hunt, finding the perfect candidate, helping someone find a great job.

Think for a moment about your favorite part of your job.

Did you say your favorite part is dealing with the hiring manager? Very few recruiters like that part—until they learn how to create a real business relationship with their hiring managers.

What has your strategy been to create that business partner relationship? Usually recruiters tell me they build credibility with their hiring managers by finding great candidates. It is an important part of your job, but it should be only **one** part of your strategy for creating a credible business partner relationship.

What are the reasons to have a multi-pronged strategy designed to help you build partnerships with your hiring managers?

First, it might take some time for you to find and get those great candidates hired. Secondly, if you don't have a great relationship with your hiring managers, the recruiting process will probably be painful. Sadly, the reality is you won't improve a relationship simply by great hires.

*Research by Bersin Deloitte Revealed a*
*Startling Recruiting Reality:*

*Strong Relationships Between Recruiter and*
*Hiring Managers Are THE Most Important Factor*
*in Recruiting Success.*

*In Fact, It was More Important than All the*
*Other 14 Factors Combined That They*
*Researched!*

When you are spending time trying to get the hiring manager to get back to you and/or the candidates, to move quickly so they don't lose the candidate, to make an offer that isn't a low ball, you're not able to spend that time finding great candidates. Think about how much time is wasted because you and the hiring manager aren't on the same page.

And in the worst cases, think about how many times you've lost a candidate because of these issues and had to start over. All that effort was wasted!

So finding great candidates is certainly necessary, but it's really just the ticket to get you into the game. There is a faster—and easier—way to build good working relationships with your hiring managers.

This is a little like trying to change the tires while the bus is roaring down the freeway. That's why I'm going to suggest you do small things first and perhaps one at a time. They will add up pretty quickly and you'll be on the way to building great relationships with your hiring managers.

Let's define what makes a great relationship. Think about the kind of relationship a trusted advisor would have with their hiring managers. What would a great relationship look like? What would be the advantages to you when you have a true business partnership with your hiring managers.

A while ago we talked about what you would like from your hiring manager. Great to think that might happen, isn't it? Imagine how much faster you would fill reqs and the time you would save when your hiring managers work with you! And the icing on the cake? You'll have more influence and credibility. People will actually start asking for your advice and collaborate with you to solve recruiting and/or hiring challenges.

Hiring managers tend to use their own measures to determine if they are happy with their recruiting function.

It's time to think about what your hiring managers want.

**Sample of a satisfaction survey**.

If you're doing satisfaction surveys at the end of your searches already, then you have some great data that you can use to build stronger relationships. The techniques we're going to talk about will help you do that faster and easier than you ever imagined.

If you're not doing surveys yet, I do NOT suggest doing a satisfaction survey just yet. Surprised?

There are two reasons I'm suggesting you hold off, or just do a casual conversation to get a sense of the areas that are bothering your hiring managers.

The first reason to hold off is the response many people have when someone asks them to do a satisfaction survey. They aren't always excited about what they may view as extra work. They also have expectations that run the gamut from "nothing is going to change" to "there must be exciting changes on the way."

The second reason is that we can probably predict pretty accurately the kinds of issues your hiring managers would say they have. In case it helps you, they are probably the universal issues we hear from in all our consulting engagements. No need to get your hiring managers to write them down and reinforce the feeling!

But since we probably already know what their main concerns will be, you can use these techniques to start fixing those concerns right now—very quietly, without any fanfare. And in a really short time you'll start to feel a very different reaction from your hiring managers.

Then, when you do start a survey process, you'll be talking to a business partner hiring manager. The feedback will be in the spirit of a "partnership." You'll hear some good news as well as some additional points to consider working out. But you'll be talking to someone who views you even better than they might right now. They just might start to see the value-add you bring to filling their positions.

When you look at a typical satisfaction survey like the one in the documents at the back, you'll see the areas that need to be considered. Pick the one or two that your hiring managers are probably most unhappy with, and that's where you start using these techniques.

One last thought on the satisfaction survey concept. I'm lucky in that I get to talk to a lot of companies about recruiting. I'm always interested in how they measure their recruiting function in terms of value. We will talk about metrics in a later technique, but here I'm talking about how companies determine if their recruiting function is doing well.

Interestingly and surprisingly to me initially, it wasn't a dollar measurement (e.g., ROI or cost to hire) nor was it a time-to-fill type of measurement. It was "How do the hiring managers feel about our recruiting team?" If the hiring managers are happy, the perceived value of the function is seen as high. And obviously the opposite is also true. Building solid business partner relationships is often neglected, misunderstood or seen as not as important as finding candidates. Yet it's a major factor in successful recruiting. (See Section: **Why Finding Great Candidates Isn't Enough**)

*When I was doing a lot of searches for a big entertainment company in Southern California, I got to spend time with the VP of Talent Acquisition, one of the most proactive, forward-thinking recruiting professionals I had ever met. She was doing things several years ago that many recruiting functions are just starting to add to their process today.*

*Expecting an interesting, forward-thinking answer, I asked her how she determined if a recruiter was doing a good job. I'll never forget her answer or my surprise. It actually is what prompted me to write these techniques down for you.*

*She said, "If the hiring managers are happy, the recruiters are doing a good job. If they aren't happy, the recruiters are not doing a good job. That's really what it boils down to." My enlightened, metrics-driven Talent Acquisition leader simply used her hiring managers' level of satisfaction to determine how a recruiter was doing. I suspect this is the measurement being used in more than one company today.*

In the next section, we'll see how some typical recruiter good intentions actually backfire and damage your credibility and influence. And what to do instead!

**NEW! Video Master Class  Epic Result Recruiting: Exactly How You Can Shatter Forever the Undeserved Stereotype of "Order Taker" and Start Having More Influence and Credibility with Your Hiring Managers**

**Check it out Here:** Or here: https://the-consultative-recruiter.teachable.com/p/how-to-leverage-ai-tools-to-become-a-consultative-recruiter

# Good Intentions That Backfire on Recruiters

## Shattering the Order Taker Stereotype: A French Fry Moment

*French Fry Moment Strategy:*
*Stay and Ask Questions to Get Clarification*
*Avoid the **OK, Go Away, Get Away!***

Often we miss an opportunity to step into a consultative role with our hiring managers in times I've come to think of as ***French Fry Moments***.

When the hiring manager says things like, "Nope, didn't like your candidates, don't like the resumes, don't think these people are right, don't want to make an offer". Don't want to do anything, basically, you are experiencing a ***French Fry Moment***.

This can be frustrating and embarrassing because we thought things were going well, and the hiring manager doesn't agree.

(I thought that name sounds like it should be a country and western song. Hence the picture. I added the "recruiter mojo" to make sure you remember you've got "mojo"!)

Understandably we may respond "okay". And then we will go away (somewhere, anywhere) because we can't wait to get away. The **OK, Go Away, Get Away**.

But, wait!

This is actually a great opportunity to demonstrate your expertise AND get the essential information to fill the position quickly. So resist the temptation to say OK and go away. Stick around to ask questions.

When you order French Fries, the order taker will typically take your order and go away. But sometimes they may ask additional questions to help you choose the right kind of Fries—curly, chili cheese, crinkle cut, steak fries, waffle fries, shoestring, etc. Or they may ask if you would like sweet potato fries, which you didn't even know were available.

Get more information so you can deliver the best candidates now that you know the details of what your hiring managers really want.

I'll give you an example.

*When I was managing a large team of virtual recruiters in Southern California for a specialized search firm that I still do some work for, Gretchen joined the team. Gretchen was a really good recruiter, but hadn't had a lot of training in these principles.*

*At the time, we're doing a search for DirecTV in a relatively new technology. And predictably, when you're doing a search for candidates in an area that's relatively new and hot, at the same time you are working in a very competitive situation.*

*Gretchen had done a really good job sourcing three very qualified, interested and affordable--which is always critical--candidates. She presented them using our structured approach to presenting candidates, and when that presentation call was over she called me so distressed—and I suspect, embarrassed as well.*

*The hiring manager thought that none of the candidates were right. As I said, Gretchen was a good recruiter, and I knew she had done great recruiting.*

*So, I said to her, "So, what did the hiring manager say?".*

*She said, "Well he just didn't think any of them were what he was looking for."*

*I said, "Do you know what he's looking for? The reasons they weren't right? Did he like any?".*

*"Oh," she said, "I didn't ask."*

What Gretchen had experienced was a **French Fry Moment**. What she did was the **OK, Go Away, Get Away**.

None of us want to disappoint our hiring managers. I think one of the worst feelings a recruiter can have is to feel their hiring manager is disappointed with them.

*He had said to her "None of these candidates are a fit, and I'm really disappointed because I thought we would be further along by now. I need to fill this position quickly."*

*She just said "**okay**" because she couldn't wait to **go away to get away** from the conversation. She couldn't wait to hang up the phone. She was embarrassed, even though she didn't have any reason to be because they were good candidates who actually did meet the requirements.*

*But because she was embarrassed, she did the **OK, Go Away, Get Away**.*

*So my question to here was, "What are you going to do now?"*

*She said, "Well, I'll just go back to sourcing."*

*"Well, what are you going to do differently?"*

*And she said, "Oh I'll just work harder and later and try to find more people."*

*When I asked, "How will these people need to differ from the ones you already presented?" she didn't know.*

A lot of times it's easier to do the **OK, Go Away, Get Away** than having to stand and ask the questions.

**Stay and ask** is your solution for success (See Time Saving Hack #3 for lots of great questions to ask).

It's a great way to step into your consultative recruiter role, save yourself a ton of time, and really help the hiring manager at the same time.

As difficult as it was, Gretchen asked the hiring manager more questions. See Bonus Report 4, especially techniques 2 and 3 for the questions she asked.

*There were interesting results when Gretchen went back to have the important conversation with the hiring manager who, during that conversation, came to these new conclusions:*

 a) *The candidates did match what he had told Gretchen he wanted, but*
 b) *He changed his mind once he saw the resumes, realizing he had not given her the appropriate set of requirements.*

*Now Gretchen knew what to look for in her next round of sourcing. If she had not gone back to ask the hiring manager the critical questions, she would have spent a lot of time looking for more candidates who looked like the ones she had already presented. Clearly that would have made for a long and painful search.*

*The next slate of presented candidates was what the hiring manager was looking for.*

*As a result, that req was filled quite quickly. The hiring manager was so pleased with Gretchen's consulting approach that he requested to work with her on several more searches.*

**NEW! Video Master Class  Epic Result Recruiting: Exactly How You Can Shatter Forever the Undeserved Stereotype of "Order Taker" and Start Having More Influence and Credibility with Your Hiring Managers**

**Check it out Here:**

Or here:
https://the-consultative-recruiter.teachable.com/p/how-to-leverage-ai-tools-to-become-a-consultative-recruiter

## How to Lose Credibility While Trying to Please Them

*Recently one of the recruiters I've been coaching shared a challenge she had with some of her hiring managers. She admitted she had created the situation when she started working with a new group of hiring managers, prompted by wanting them to like her.*

*So in those first few weeks, she gave them special attention, often neglecting other hiring managers so she could spend more time on the reqs for the new group, let the new hiring managers do things that actually made her job more difficult, and stayed up late trying to source more and more candidates for them.*

*That had backfired big time.*

Surprise! Now they expect that level of service all time, and when they don't get it from her (or you), guess what? They are unhappy! They **don't** say, "Well, we got special service in the beginning so it makes sense we don't get that kind of special service going forward. But no problem because we really like our recruiter!"

At one time, probably all of us have tried building a business relationship by trying to be liked. So we learned first-hand that a few days or few weeks of special treatment is absolutely not the best way to build your reputation as a consultative recruiter.

How do you know where to draw the line?

You know that feeling of "I'll do this for them just this time. I'm sure it will help build a relationship with them." or "They will appreciate the extra attention I'm giving them. I'll just do it for now and then turn it over to them. They will respect me for this."?

That's your signal that you should not do what you're thinking of doing!

Have the courage to stay in consultative recruiter mode. Resist sliding into people please mode.

## How "Under Promising and Over Delivering" Actually Hurts Your Credibility

When we are trying to figure out how demonstrate our value-add and build strong business partnerships with our hiring managers, we may resort to old advice: Under Promise and Over Deliver.

That doesn't advance your trusted advisor reputation. Even worse, it actually quickly and significantly damages your credibility.

You know that feeling of "this will impress them" or "they will think I'm great when they see this."? I don't know about you, but I've often thought that.

When you do, however, that's your signal that you should not do it what you're thinking of doing!

The reason this doesn't work in your favor is because people come to distrust whatever you say. And it happens very quickly. (Check out the first bullet under **5 Ways to Build & Reinforce Your Consultative Recruiter Image)**

They don't know you worked hard to deliver early (or more candidates than promised or anything else where you have under-promised). They come to expect that any timeline you give them will actually be shorter. They automatically discount what you say.

If you promise to get something to them in two days and you send it at the end of the first day, what happens? They may or may not say anything. They probably will NOT say "Oh, you are wonderful. You must have worked hard to get this to me so much faster. Thank you!"

How do I know that?

*I had been engaged to do a search for a technology company which a widely-acknowledged difficult CEO who was my client. The formal launch meeting (using the launch form you can find in the special report How to Have Your Best Search Ever) went well.*

*When we were done, I went over next steps and the timing of them. As I always do, I gave myself enough time to write a great posting based on what he had told me. Never works to cut that time too tight for yourself.*

*So I promised to get it to him in two days—absolutely under promising because typically I like to have three. But did I stick to that commitment? NO!*

*After working hard to create a great posting, I did something I will never do again. I sent him the posting draft in at the end of the first day—which had been a lot of work!. I heard a little voice say "Probably not a good idea." But I successfully ignored it.*

*Reason? I have to admit I was hoping he would say "Wow, what a great job. And you got it done early. You're amazing."*

*What did he say? "OK, thanks."*

*What also happened? Every time I made a prediction of how long something would take, he just ignored my timeline. He really didn't believe me because I had thought I was doing a good thing early in our relationship.*

*It took some time to rebuild my credibility. And you can probably imagine one way I did it was to never under-promise and over-deliver again!*

# Technique 1: Creating a Business Partnership

**The Elephant in the Room**

An Executive Search company I worked for was engaged by a large healthcare system to tell them how to improve their recruiting function. Basically, the SVP HR and many of the hiring managers felt it was "badly broken." I cannot tell you how many times we've heard that. Often those managers just throw up their hands and say there must not be any way to make things better.

In our consulting engagements we almost always find the elephant in the room is this: The recruiting function is misunderstood and often treated with a vendor-like relationship rather than a business partnership relationship. There, that's out in the open.

Managers do have a sense that recruiting is necessary, but it often is so painful for them to deal with recruiting that they will do anything to avoid having to do it. And they minimize their interaction with the recruiting team to avoid what they perceive as a troubled relationship.

We found in this organization:

- The recruiters and hiring managers followed a "process"—it just wasn't the same process for each group.
- Recruiters felt unappreciated and undervalued.
- Hiring managers felt the recruiters didn't understand the pressures the hiring managers were experiencing. They also felt that recruiting was not the hiring manager's job.
- Recruiters felt the hiring managers were out of touch with the candidate marketplace and that the hiring managers did not do what they needed to do to win the candidates.
- The communication between the managers and recruiters was nearly non-existent and certainly dysfunctional.

And the piece that was overlooked? The recruiters were often bringing in some great candidates.

So after discussions with the managers, senior management and the recruiting team, we were able to help them agree on a process, open the lines of communication, and set appropriate expectations. In other words, they started to function as business partners.

Take a moment now and answer this question: If you and your hiring managers were really working together right now as business partners, what would that look like? Which of the following items would you want your hiring manager to do?

- Take the time up front to discuss all aspects of the position and search with you
- Respect the fact you are talking to candidates every day and you understand the marketplace today.
- Value your advice on what constitutes a competitive salary, which are the best candidates, what is the best recruiting strategy to follow.
- Give you timely feedback on resumes/candidates you've submitted without having to chase them down.
- Not blow off interviews or want the candidate to be interviewed by waaaay too many people.

- Work with you to create a compelling candidate experience.
- Give you interview feedback about a candidate beyond the words "not a fit".
- Respect your advice about what an offer needs to be and how quickly they need to make a decision so as to not lose the candidate.
- In other words, partner with you as a trusted advisor!

You may be just like me and nearly every other recruiter I've talked to. We all want to feel valued for the contribution we make. We want to feel we're a part of a team with a common goal for the good of the company, the hiring manager, the candidates and ourselves.

We provide a critical service to our companies and want people to appreciate that service enough to partner with us so we can all do our jobs well. Be nice if they just started appreciating us right now, wouldn't it? But if history is any teacher, that probably isn't going to happen spontaneously.

Waiting for the other person to change is easier, but how's that working so far?

So let's talk about how to use some simple techniques to start getting the results you want--because it is possible.

That's the good news. Now the bad news. You have to use these techniques in order to benefit from them. I personally feel that just buying the treadmill should be enough!! But it never was. Of course, it was a convenient place to hang my clothes. But until I actually used it, nothing happened.

Now for more good news. Actually using the treadmill really meant adding another to-do to my already overbooked schedule. But to be successful with this approach to building a better business partnership, you don't need to add anything else to what you're doing.

You just need to replace what isn't working with what will work. And I will point out both of those things so it will be easy to see what isn't working, why it isn't working, and what to do instead.

In a recent workshop showing these techniques to a group of recruiters, one of them had to leave mid-way through to take a call with a hiring manager. She didn't look eager to have that conversation.

When she came back she was beaming. She couldn't wait to report that she had tried one of the techniques we had just discussed, and was blown away with how effective it had been in changing the hiring manager's behavior. You can take control—get what you want—and get it fast! And you can start NOW!

This is a good time for you to decide what you want your relationship with your managers to look like. What parts of the process do you want them to participate in? How will they treat you? How will they treat your candidates? How will they—and you—feel when a hire is made?

We'll go into this in more detail with the next technique, and you'll see why it's so essential to start with the end in mind.

There is one other thing I would like you to do as we end this discussion. I'm going to ask you to think of yourself as a trusted advisor and business partner to your hiring managers—now. Not a recruiter but a consultant/advisor whose expertise and specialty are recruiting.

Your hiring managers may have more business experience, or more education or a higher title than you do. But the one thing they don't have is your expertise and skill in recruiting. They need you. They may not realize and/or acknowledge that just yet, but they will!

As you move through these techniques, make sure you keep thinking of yourself as a business partner to your hiring managers. That is a great way to become the consultative recruiter you are very capable of being.

In the next technique, you will learn the ins and outs of a foundational piece of your consultative recruiting toolkit. You may be as surprised as I was when I started using this technique. Examples of it are throughout the book, and lots in Bonus Reports. So you can start right away. Enjoy!

# Technique 2: Secret Strategy to Build Influence and Trust

In my first recruiting position at Deloitte & Touche, I learned a lot about consulting strategies. I was amazed at how effective consultants were able to do two important things at the same time:

- Get the information they need to be successful, and
- Build their reputation as a true consultant and get relative strangers to trust them

How do they do that? If you're like I was at that time, the answer—and the simplicity of that answer-- may really surprise you.

**They ask a lot of questions.**

That was certainly contrary to how I thought success was achieved. I thought it was the one who had all the answers was the one who other people saw as the expert. What I learned there is that the one with the good questions is the one who controls the conversation, is actually seen as the expert by the expertise demonstrated in their questions, and ultimately determines the success of any project.

---

*The one with the good questions is the one who controls the conversation and is seen as the expert by the expertise demonstrated by their questions.*

---

Of course that was a little disappointing to me because, at that time, I kind of prided myself on "having all the answers." Of course I didn't have all the answers. But I drove myself and everyone around me crazy trying to pretend that I did indeed "know it all".

So I thought it was worth a try. Maybe asking questions would be a good strategy for me to get the same two results as the consultants I was learning from.

Of course, the reality is that when you ask lots of good questions, you end up with all the answers—or least enough of them to be successful. When you ask good questions, people don't question your expertise—they actually start to see you in a new light. A favorable light, I might add.

## *A Little Concerned About Asking a Lot of Questions?*

As children, many of us were told we shouldn't ask a lot of questions. I'm going to have to ask you to violate Mom's advice.

If you are like most of us, you may be a little wary of asking questions because:

- I'm already supposed to know this.
- If I keep asking questions, won't people think I don't know my job?

- I hate to ask a question and let people know I'm confused.
- It will be so embarrassing to ask a "stupid" question.
- Etc., etc., etc.

These are concerns are valid, and I want to help you with them throughout this book. I'm going to show you how to ask a question in a way that significantly lowers the likelihood anyone will think it is "stupid."

We all know the saying, "There is no such thing as a stupid question."

Well if that's true, how come I've felt stupid asking certain questions? So I will share techniques that help you ask any question in a way that sounds both "smart" and "interesting". They will truly position you as the consultative recruiter. Interestingly, they also point out your expertise and value-add!

One thing to remember is that if the question gets the other person to talk about themselves or anything else they enjoy talking about, you and the question are probably not judged at all.

The other person is talking about something important to them and is noticing that you had the good judgment to ask them for their thoughts, opinion, perspective, etc. Who doesn't like to have someone ask for that?

And another big bonus? Questions are actually a great way to demonstrate expertise, by the way, and you'll see that as we go through this.

## How to Make Questions Your Secret Strategy

Let me share with you a concept that I love. It was totally new to me and it may be to you also: **you lead the conversation by asking questions**. I've found it is actually the best way to take control because it doesn't sound like a lecture or excuses or things your hiring managers don't want to hear again.

A lot of times, we think that the way to talk about what we know, to demonstrate our value add is to explain it. The reality is that you actually can lead people more by asking them questions.

Here is what one recruiter reported as an example of what you can expect by asking questions:

*"I did what you suggested and asked my hiring manager some questions when he told me he had decided not to move ahead with a candidate.*

*We actually had a great conversation.*

*He said he appreciated my asking questions about his decision and admitted he hadn't thought it through. He decided the candidate really was a good fit and decided to make them an offer! Now I have a great time-to-fill stat on this req.*

*He ended by encouraging me to keep asking questions to help him with his thinking. This is high praise from any hiring manager here, but I had struggled with him because I felt he was always questioning my ability. I will add that he is the only hiring manager who has ever made me cry!"*

Recruiter would like to remain anonymous (I'm sure you can see why!)

When you ask questions, you are the one driving the conversation, and ironically, at the same time, good questions demonstrate your expertise.

*If you want to lead the conversation, ask questions. The one asking the question is controlling the direction of the discussion.*

*You actually change what someone is thinking about by asking a question.*

*And you often find you can gently lead people to the conclusion you wanted them to reach just by letting them answer your carefully crafted questions. Try it! You'll love the results!*

The whole concept of asking questions to build influential relationships is leveraging this reality:

*People don't have a long attention span. The best way to get their attention and keep them engaged in the conversation is to **ask them questions.***

**Guidelines about how to ask questions.**

In the world today--our goldfish world--if you're just telling people things--hiring managers, your boss, your business partners-- have you noticed that they don't always pay attention?

I've learned that just because someone's looking at you doesn't mean they're listening. Even if they are listening, it doesn't mean that you've convinced them to your way of thinking. If we want to be effective, just telling people isn't going to work. **To tell won't sell.**

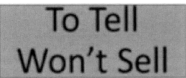

Now, you and I know that what you're talking about is really important information. And we know that if people would listen, take your advice, and follow your guidance, hiring would be a lot better. You're right!

I've never met a recruiter who didn't have a lot of really great ideas on how to improve things in the recruiting and hiring strategies of their company.

But it's how we present that information that matters. Remember, to tell won't sell.

If people won't pay attention to things that they perceive as boring, what will NOT be boring to them?

---

*The mind will not pay attention to boring things.*
*John Medina, Brain Rules*

---

Why does that matter? Because we need them to be engaged in the conversations with us. It's hard to be effective as a trusted advisor when people don't even listen to your advice, much less actually TAKE it!!

Here is the beautiful thing about what we're doing here. You can build your reputation, improve your results, be seen as a trusted advisor, simply by paying attention to the things that are not boring to them.

How do you do that? By making the conversation about them and what they're thinking.

When you ask a question, we're leveraging the goldfish world by changing our conversation to something that will be interesting to them—themselves and what they are thinking.

We're leveraging the reality that *to tell won't sell*. We are asking questions, and we are asking the kinds of questions that direct the conversation. I've got lots of examples for you, and you'll get new results right away.

But even so, you may be concerned because it feels like you've given up control, right?

The reality is, you are controlling the conversational direction. Even better, because you have the expertise, you know where you want to get them and the information you want them to have.

When you use this strategy, there's no need for a "pushback". It's just a nice, gentle and often invisible controlling of the conversation. It is the easiest and fastest way to build credibility and have more influence.

I always love getting my own way, which is what you will get many, many, many times when you use this approach.

### The Recruiter Who Thought "Just Tell Them" Was a Good Tactic

*At one of my corporate trainings, as we were discussing the reality and power of asking questions, one recruiter vehemently disagreed. Joe said, "I don't want to let my hiring managers control when they do things. I just tell them what I need. That works for me. And my hiring managers like and respect me."*

*Kind of makes sense, right? It's easier and feels like you're taking control when you just tell people what you need and when you need it. But how often does that really work?*

*First, just "telling" isn't a relationship-building strategy.*

*Of course, being a consultative recruiter isn't about being a door mat or people pleaser. It's about building a relationship of credibility and influence. When you create win-win resolutions, you are more likely to get what you need when you need it. And you will have the credibility to get people to follow your guidance and advice.*

*Second, what he didn't realize is how people were reacting to his tactic of "just telling."*

*When I had done the pre-workshop debrief with his manager, she had a very different perspective of his effectiveness and ability to have credible relationships with his hiring managers.*

*She reported that, while he was filling positions, his managers were actually complaining about him—to her and a lot! (For more perspective on this reality, please read the Bonus Section "Why Finding Great Candidates Isn't Enough".)*

*It seems they resented his dictating to them and felt he was being pushy. They didn't like working with him, felt times to fill were too long, and just generally had lots of complains about him—some of which were probably not deserved, but...*

*So while he was filling positions, he was not viewed positively. He certainly was not building relationships nor positioning himself as a trusted advisor and consultative recruiter.*

*And his tactics were resulting in very long times to fill and complaints that were driving his manager crazy! To tell won't sell!*

*Bottom line? Joe's manager was unhappy with him and tired of the complaints..*

*Sadly, Joe was sure his way was THE way. While he kept filling positions, it continued to take a long time to fill those positions.*

*And his hiring managers never changed their opinion of him!*

*What was the impact on his career? He missed out on promotions, was never invited by his hiring managers to critical business meetings, was not asked his advice on hiring, and was generally treated like an order-taker.*

I feel badly for Joe, who did have the makings of a great consultative recruiter—but he had to be willing to do a few things a little differently to truly reach that potential.

## 3 Keys for Your Questions: Simple Changes that Build Credibility and Influence

1. **Know when to stop talking!**

Here is the first key technique for success when you ask your questions.

*Ask the question and then stop talking!*

This is really critical when you ask a question, especially in the world today where people don't pay attention for very long.

You must create some silence for the other person to think about their answer. That silence should happen right after you ask the question.

What many of us do is ask a question and then keep talking.

If you ask a question and then talking, they're just going latch onto something you say and answer you. They are ready to answer when you ask the question. When you keep talking, they lose interest. Think about what you would do in their shoes.

The reason is that we haven't really given them a chance to think about it and make a decision. No decision—no commitment.

A lot of times recruiters will say--I used to do this too—"So when do you think you're going to make a decision about who you're going to hire?" Or, "When are we going to be able to move forward with the candidate?" Or, "When you're going to interview the candidates we already have?"

Those are important questions to help keep moving toward a faster fill of your req.

But then we don't stop talking and let them think long enough to come up with their answer.

So, I would say, "When do you think you can make a decision about which of these candidates you want to interview?" I might pause a nanosecond.

Then I would say things like "*Because if we don't get back to them, we're going to lose them. They're highly competitive. This is a tight market. Things are happening--blah, blah, blah.* "

Now it's starting to sound like a lecture.

While what I was saying was true, the problem is people a) didn't really want to hear it and b) it doesn't result in a thoughtful decision or any real commitment to that decision.

**The really critical part is for you to ask and then be quiet.**

I know you want to offer alternatives. You want to explain why their answer is important. You want to give them ideas or suggestions. Stifle all of those impulses and just wait for them to answer you.

It is really important that you stop talking and then wait for them to answer. Don't ask if they understand the question. Don't ask anything.

Ask one question at a time. This is really key. **Ask one question at a time and stop talking**.

2.   **Ask questions they can answer**

*Ask "Small" Questions—Meaning Questions
They Can Actually Answer!*

It took me an embarrassingly long time to figure this out–just because we call them "hiring managers," it doesn't mean they are good at it or even like it!

They may not know how to interview or assess candidates. I've been amazed at how many TA leaders tell me their hiring managers have never had any interviewing training at all. That can make your job even more challenging.

So often the reason you don't get good feedback about candidates is because hiring managers are not good at evaluating candidates in any useful way or giving you a thoughtful answer to certain questions.

For example, let's say the hiring manager has interviewed several great candidates, but tells you, "I'm not ready to make an offer." And you thought that the req was about to be closed. You thought you'd found the perfect candidate (finally!), and the hiring manager was happy (finally!), and that we were going to make an offer (finally!).

Hiring manager says, "Oh, I'm not ready to make an offer."

Recruiters often tell me when this happens, they ask "Well, when do you think you'll be ready to make an offer?" or "Why not?"

The problem with the first question is a) the hiring manager may not be sure of the reasons they are not ready to move forward or what it will take to be "ready" and b) you don't know what it is about the current candidates that resulted in the hiring manager not feeling ready to forward. How can you set your recruiting strategy to go forward without specifics.

Of course, the problem with the second question is all of the above plus it's a "why" question.

So when you get vague responses like these that give you no direction whatsoever, you have to ask smaller questions—questions they can actually answer.

For example, questions like, "Has something changed in the business so that isn't appropriate to make an offer at this point? Have you changed your mind about what qualifications you're looking for in candidates? Do we need to change the requirements or anything else about the position?" can be useful to help the hiring manager give you useful information?

If the answers to these questions are basically "no", then you need to ask questions about the candidates.

For some incredibly useful small questions, read about Gretchen's situation in the section, The French Fry Moment. Also refer to Bonus Report 4, techniques 2 and 3, for more "small questions" that will help your hiring manager think all this through. You'll be amazed at what might happen.

Here is another example of how small questions make all the difference:

> The recruiting firm I worked for was engaged to fill a senior sales position for a national landscaping company. I was conducting the launch meeting on a call with the company CEO and the CEO of our recruiting firm.
>
> One question I always ask is "What is **the most important thing** this person should do?" (small question. When you ask for "the most important thing" or "the one thing" etc., you are asking small questions. Asking for "the one" or "most important" gets much better information than a vague big question like What does this person do?)
>
> The CEO answered "Provide good customer service."
>
> The CEO of our firm asked, "Why is that important?" (big question and a "why" question—aughhh!)
>
> Client CEO replied, "It's what we pride ourselves on." Sounds good but still very vague. What does he really mean?

*Every company could say that. But what The Cheesecake Factory or PFChangs considers their definition is very different that that that used by Children's Hospital or Southern California Auto Club. I know because I've done searches for all of them, and the words they use to describe their "good customer service" are all very different.*

*Our CEO moved on to another question, and the "good customer service" discussion was done. It's tempting to do the OK, Go Away Get Away when you get this kind of answer. Asking the next question is really important to both get good information and build your consultant image.)*

*As you probably can guess, as soon as it seemed appropriate, I went back to the "good customer service" response, asking:*

1. *"How do you define 'good customer service'?"?"*(A question you might be reluctant to ask because doesn't everyone know what that means? Having done searches for companies in hospitality, retail, technology and many others, I've learned that every company say they want to provide good customer service but they all use different criteria and words to define what it means to them.

   What we are after is to understand the words the CEO uses. It makes a difference when you are talking to your hiring manager about candidates. It also tells you if the hiring manager has thought this through or is just saying the words because they sound like words he should say. And another bonus is that it will help you see if your candidate is likely to be a hit with the CEO. )

2. *"What is the reason that is the most important thing to you?"* (Again, perhaps a question you may be reluctant to ask. Seems like everyone should know the answer to that, right? But if the CEO is real about wanting to provide good customer service, that can be a powerful selling point to the right kind of potential candidates. And equally important is that it may turn off candidates who aren't customer service focused—saving you from wasting time with them.*)*

3. *"How do you determine if the candidate you're interviewing really understands and delivers "good customer service."* (To help the CEO feel comfortable sharing this information, I assured him that I would not be coaching candidates in any way. I explain the reason we never coach candidates is because the candidate they interview on Thursday may not be the candidate who shows up on Monday if they have been coached. You may think that is something your hiring managers understand but saying it can be a powerful consultant strategy.*)*

If you're thinking this takes a lot of time and your hiring manager might be exasperated with your questions, let me share a different perspective.

First, if your hiring manager is serious about something they say is important, they will appreciate you are wanting to know more. After all, how often does someone express real interest in something that is important to us? And third, you can more easily spot the candidates your hiring manager is really hoping to find. Faster closes and happier hiring managers!!

Secondly, it clearly it takes longer to read the above questions and notes than it will ever take to ask them ☺

## Why You Should Never ask "Why"

For many years I have been studying how language can influence, modify, as well as reinforce, behavior. I know you recognize that's one of the key concepts we've been talking about in all these techniques.

---

*Avoid Asking Any Question that*
*Starts with "WHY"!*

*It Puts People on the Defensive and Makes*
*Them Feel Judged.*

---

Long ago I heard an interesting statement: "The quality of your life reflects the quality of your questions."

While I didn't really understand it at the time, I finally realized that when I ask good questions, I get good information. Everything in life, especially relationships, is better when I have good information on which to base my actions.

As you read the questions I have written in all of these strategies, you may have realized that none of them start with the word "why."

If there is one thing I had to choose as the biggest and best way to build strong relationships with your hiring managers (and raise your candidate assessment skills at the same time) it would be to never ask a question that starts with "why."

Spoiler Alert: This may be one of the most difficult changes I ask you to consider.

## WHY?

"Why did you tell the candidate they would be coming back for another interview, even though you don't think they are a fit for your position?" "Why are you rejecting this candidate?" "Why are you interested in this candidate who doesn't seem to meet your requirements?"

*The recruiting firm where I managed a virtual team was engaged by a long-time client to do a senior management position. After the CEO interviewed our first 2 candidates, both of them told me the CEO had told them they would be moving forward to the next step.*

*When I talked to the VP HR, she told me the CEO had not really liked either of the candidates. She didn't understand why the CEO had told them about moving forward. She had asked him "why" he just said "I didn't really like them."*

*I asked him "What prompted you to tell both of them they would be moving forward?"*

*He replied, "I didn't know what else to tell them, and I didn't want to disappoint them."*

*Once we understood that, we could give him a face-saving and appropriate way to end interviews if he didn't feel the candidate was fit. It made him feel more comfortable with interviewing. Plus it was a wonderful indication of how he cared about people.*

*While it may seem like a minor thing, it did strengthen our relationship with him. He subsequently asked me several questions about the best way to handle certain interview situations.*

On the surface, asking a "why" question is innocent enough. Look deeper and you'll find some real problems with the word "Why?".

First, it tends to put people on the defensive. "Why?" especially in the context of an inquiring discussion, can give a hint of disagreement and/or judgment. To the person you've asked "Why" there will be a subtle feeling of being put on the spot and being asked to justify what they did. Justification is almost always different than explanation.

I know we don't intend to create this feeling with our hiring managers. But this automatic reaction to "why" really happens to all of us.

Unfortunately, ever since childhood, when we hear "Why did you do that?" we start looking for cover (the best cover usually being making something up). So it's a matter of conditioning.

We have learned to over-rely on that particular type of question. It's an old habit, a reflex reaction, and frankly the easy (and perhaps lazy) way to ask questions. We don't need to think about the information we really want. We expect to get it from that old yet inefficient standby: WHY.

Secondly, "Why?" questions usually do not fulfill the "small questions they can answer" guideline. They often are just unanswerable questions, especially if the person being asked isn't really clear about their motives. In that case, you won't get an answer much deeper than, "Because I wanted to!" or "Well, it seemed like a good idea at the time." You will get an answer, but it won't be the great information you'll get when you change your question.

Lastly, a reason that makes perfect sense to your hiring manager may make not a single iota of sense to you. You'll end up frustrated with your hiring manager because their answer doesn't make sense to you.

In fact, an accurate translation of a WHY question might be, "I don't have the foggiest idea why you did such a dumb thing, but if you'll explain it to me, I'll listen and then tell you why you're wrong."

I believe any question that starts with "Why" should be rephrased. Why? Because as we just explored, 'why' is often a lazy question that puts your hiring managers on the defensive and can force them to justify their opinions, not expand upon a point of view.

Of course "WHY" is an easy question to ask. It is often used as a short cut when you're seeking speedy answers.

In reality, what you really want to know is "what's the intention or goal?", "what's the reason?", "what's the motivation?", "what is your thought about that?" etc.

If you will start to replace "WHY" with these phrases, you will be amazed at the richness of the answer you get. You get better and more information because people don't, at that very subliminal level, go on the defensive.

Try this in any of your conversations. You'll be delighted with how much more information you get—you'll feel you're finally getting the real story. And people will be sharing information with you they may not have shared before—because no one asked them the question the way you did.

Bonus: they are essentially talking about themselves, and that fits the "Not Boring" requirement.

Try an experiment just to see how incredible it is to ask questions with anything other than "WHY." Take any questions and rather than ask it as I've given it to you, ask it by starting with "Why".

Notice the reaction and the information from the person you've asked. Now ask the question the way we discussed. Or craft the question your way—just without "why".

Think about what you want to know—what their intention was, what was the compelling reason they did something, what they were hoping to accomplish, what their motivation was, etc. And phrase the question to reflect what it is specifically that you want to know.

Same question—almost—yet you will get much richer information from the WHY question.

As I warned you earlier: Getting the "WHY" habit out of my questions was probably the most difficult change for me to make. Frankly didn't happen overnight. But every time I ask a WHY question and get defensive reaction or skimpy or even totally useless answer, I'm reminded of why (sorry) it's worth it to make the effort.

Then I ask the question again and realize how much more useful information I got because I was willing to make the effort to rephrase the question. It's truly worth it.

Try it and let me know how it goes!

On to the next technique that is all about knowing what is most important to focus on. We'll talk about where you are now and where you want to go.

It's like that story where one person asks: ***Can you tell me how to get to Phoenix?*** The other person says yes, but there is one critical piece of information I need: ***Where are you now?***

If you don't know what they are thinking now, it's very difficult to get them where you want them to go.

This may also be why **You can lead a horse to water but can't make them drink.**

Probably no one bothered to check if the horse was thirsty.

Of course, I'm not thinking of your hiring managers as horses, but there is a great hint in that story that can help you and hopefully give you patience to find out exactly what your hiring manager is thinking, wanting, worried about, etc.

# Technique 3: How to Make Sure They Will Love You When it's Over

So where to start?

Spend just a few seconds thinking about the behavior implied by the title Trusted Advisor. Or recruiting consultant. Or whatever term feels most appropriate for you.

The essential thing here is that you are creating a new image and thinking in new expanded ways. Once you've decided how you want to be and how you want your hiring manager relationships to be, it's just a matter of using these techniques. If you haven't taken that first step to create a new image, these techniques will still work but it will take longer to build your reputation as a trusted advisor.

Look at the survey sample at the back (or one you already have). Identify where can you make small incremental improvements that will have the biggest impact—this will help you right away to create a business partner relationship.

What would your hiring managers most like to see improved?

Surprisingly, when you think of their issues, you may find they mirror your issues. It may turn out you and they are more alike than either of you realize.

Let's take the plunge. Pick one or two hiring managers to try out these techniques. Of course then the questions is, do I pick the one I have the best relationship with or do I pick the one with whom I have the worst relationship?

*Madeline was a recruiter I coached a while ago. She decided to start with her most critical and difficult hiring manager. She had just gotten a requisition for an accounting manager position. Things had gone pretty badly the last time she had filled a similar position for this manager.*

*Both the CFO to whom the hiring manager reported and the hiring manager had been pretty vocal in their criticism of her recruiting. They felt the previous search had taken too long and were convinced they should have seen more and higher quality candidates.*

*I'm not sure I would have been as gutsy as Madeline was, but she decided to try out her new techniques with these two!*

*As she reviewed the satisfaction survey I provided, she identified where she thought the hiring manager and the CFO would give her low marks. She realized they were items that all related to the fact they did not spend time at the beginning of the search defining the position duties and the kinds of candidates they wanted to see.*

*Until now, the CFO and the hiring manager had been "too busy" to spend any time with her when the previous search had started.*

*So she realized that if she started using the techniques to get that up front meeting, they were going to be happier at the end with the whole search process. And they wouldn't even know what had changed!*

Madeline's story continues. Keep reading.

*Rather than ask outright for a meeting to discuss the position, her first step was to use the approach in the next technique. She launched her campaign to get them to see her as a trusted advisor, a recruiting consultant, which is what our next technique is all about.*

Creating a business partnership doesn't happen overnight. But it will happen. The good news is you'll start to see small changes right away. That's how you know its working!

Remember you're the recruiting expert. You've decided to take control and create this business partner relationship for the good of all concerned. You'll have a great time as a trusted advisor!

So pick which hiring manager you want to start with—where are you going to begin trying out these techniques? How would that hiring manager respond to the questions on the satisfaction survey? Think for a moment about the kind of relationship you would like to have with that hiring manager.

With the end in mind, we can figure out how to get there.

# Technique 4: A Quick Path to Build Your Image as A business Partner

**How a question about a light switch launched my first career.**

Let me share this secret right away—just because I hate waiting to tell you the good stuff. **The easiest and fastest way to build your business partner relationships is to ask good questions**. I hope you aren't disappointed that the answer isn't something more complicated.

And the questions can be very simple.

---

*You don't need to know a lot about the business in order to be viewed as a business partner. What you need to do is ask questions—and be genuinely interested in the answers.*

---

*A couple of years ago we were doing some prep work in advance of a recruiter training workshop in a large medical device company. One of the major recruiter complaints was that the hiring managers would not give them time at the beginning of a search. We picked one recruiter and asked to speak to his most difficult hiring manager. NOTE: I don't always recommend starting with the most difficult! I'm actually not as gutsy as Madeline.*

*When we got on the phone, it was clear the hiring manager was not planning to enjoy the conversation. He immediately repeated what he had told us when the call was scheduled--he only had 15 minutes. Typically we like to spend approximately an hour gathering all the upfront information necessary for a successful search.*

*So our first question was: "Tell us about what is happening in your business unit. What are you doing that you are excited about?"*

*And 20 minutes later he was still sharing—with excitement and enthusiasm. After he wound down (reluctantly!), we were able to ask the rest of our questions about the position, what kind of experience he wanted candidates to have, initial screening questions he wanted them to have answered before he saw them, and much more!*

*After the call, the recruiter called me immediately and said "Oh my gosh. I never had a conversation that long with him before. And I found out so much more about him and his business. It will be easy now for me to identify good candidates, to sell them on the position, and really make this a success."*

How did this happen? It all started with a simple question about something near and dear to the hiring manager's heart—his business and what he was excited about.

If you get to ask only one question, ask one similar to that. It will open the door to so much information for you – in a way the hiring manager will truly enjoy.

**How my question about a light switch built a fruitful relationship**

*I learned this in a somewhat round-about way long ago when I was brand new in my first job after college. The VP of Engineering stopped by to welcome me to the company. He stayed a little longer and chatted a bit—maybe recognizing how nervous I was. And then I nearly died when I heard myself say "So maybe you can help me understand how that light switch works. I've never understood that."*

*I really didn't understand how a light switch worked, but yikes what a stupid question to ask such an important guy. I was pretty sure I'd be fired immediately. He surely wouldn't bother to spend any more time with me.*

*And he spent the next 30 minutes explaining the light switch (not advanced technology I grant you), then how electricity worked, then how computers used the 1-0 combination, and more that I don't understand to this day.*

*I had unknowingly tapped into something that was near and dear to his electrical engineering heart, and he just loved to talk about it.*

*My boss walked by my office several times during that 30 minutes. He later told me he thought something awful must be happening. He had never seen the VP spend that much time with a new hire, and figured I was being fired. In all honesty, he was probably worried he would get in trouble for having even hired me!*

*That simple question and ensuing conversation was the beginning of a great business relationship for me. That VP continued to help and mentor me for the twelve years I worked there, and I owe my success in that company to his partnership with me.*

---

*Even the busiest person will love to answer a question about something important to them, such as their business or function.*

---

Be a little smart about picking the time and place, and you'll have a business relationship in the making.

**The only caveat is that you must care.** If you don't, people will pick up on the fact you're pretending. It will feel manipulative, and you will damage any relationship you already have.

Be fascinated with what is happening with your hiring manager's business or functions. Care about what keeps them up at night. Get excited about the things that excite them. Enjoy your newly forming business partner relationships. Knowing these things is the foundation of your trusted advisor reputation.

As you start to enjoy your new relationships and learn interesting things about your company, your hiring managers, etc., you will now be in a position to start building a real business partnership. The chances the hiring manager will spend time with you when the requisition is first opened have just increased exponentially!

Set a goal to have this kind of conversation with one hiring manager a day or a week—whatever fits your schedule and situation. Ask them if they would be open to having a cup of coffee with you to talk about these things because you really want to know. Stop by their office and see if they have a few minutes to bring you up to speed on what's happening with their business. Find what ways work best in your environment, and go get 'em!

*That's how Madeline got the CFO and hiring manager to agree to spend more time with her at the beginning of the search. She happened to be in the elevator one day with the CFO and asked him how things were going with the business. What trends was he seeing, etc.?*

*Recruiters don't often have these kinds of conversations, yet they can be real relationship-starters! So you can probably guess that when Madeline asked to schedule enough time for a true launch meeting, they both were willing participants!*

*So after she had her very effective launch conversation, she and I created a candidate-centric posting. Her hiring manager made a few edits but really liked it—and the effort Madeline has put in to write it.*

*It was still a difficult search with a hiring manager out of touch with the realities of recruiting in a competitive candidate market for a company that many people had ever heard of.*

*So yes there were still challenges. But Madeline continued to be fierce in applying the CR techniques.*

*As she continued to build on the relationship that all started with a small question, she kept asking the critical small questions that uncovered what the hiring manager was really thinking.*

*Every time she did that, she was strengthening the partnerships with her hiring manager and demonstrating her expertise and value add in a very non-pushback way. And, yes, filled the position much faster this time!*

Now please go to the next technique where I'll share some of the secret questions that will get you really good information about what the hiring manager wants, and at the same time, further build your business partnership with them.

# Technique 5: How to Get the Meeting

We've all been there as recruiters. We have a new requisition, and now we would like to get some information from the hiring manager. Don't worry; in the technique after this one I'll share some essential questions to help you get that information while building your business partner relationship at the same time.

But first we need to get the hiring manager to agree to spend some time discussing the position.

In addition, if you look at the manager survey from a few techniques ago, you'll see how much depends on your getting good information up front in a search--which I am sure is not news to you.

So it would seem to be intuitively obviously that the better the information up front, the more successful the entire search will be. Yet so many times the hiring manager will not spend the time it takes to give the recruiter what they need.

So everyone, including the candidates, all suffer as a result. Yet the recruiter is often the one who has to work so hard to make up for not having all the information. And of course the *time to fill* statistics are still running.

So we need to come up with strategies for those times when the hiring manager won't take the time to give us the information necessary.

---

*The key to success here is to help the hiring manager understand how it is in their best interest to spend this time with you.*

---

We'll discuss some ways you can "encourage" the hiring manager to take time for the meeting. Again, I know the importance of this seems so obvious to us as recruiters. We could easily say "it shouldn't be necessary for me to make a business case about why the hiring manager should spend time with me at the beginning of a search."

True, but if you're waiting in vain (and frustration) for hiring managers to agree to meet with you, let's try something different. If you were thinking "well, it's our process and they should follow it" or anything along those lines, I totally understand. At the same time we have to decide that if what we're doing so far isn't working, we have to change it.

*The corporate recruiter at one of our clients told me she would simply tell the hiring manager that if they didn't have time to meet with her when the requisition was approved, she would not do any work on it until they did meet with her. It got her the meeting but at a cost.*

*As you can imagine, it didn't do much to create a business partner relationship with her hiring managers. It made them feel they were being bullied—and they still didn't see why the meeting was necessary.*

Think of every situation as an opportunity to build your relationship and credibility with the hiring managers. This approach will help you come up with positive ways to get your hiring managers to cooperate with you.

So the key here, and in many other situations as well, is to make it obvious to the hiring manager why meeting with you is in their best interest—and not by blackmailing them!

**List the advantages the hiring manager will experience by having that upfront meeting with you.** These will include things such as:

- Ensure the hiring manager and you are on the same page which will save time and money (to say nothing of keeping frustration levels low!)
- Make sure you're screening candidates for the things that are important to the hiring manager.
- And the best part is that both you and the hiring manager will be defining success at the beginning. It's much easier to be successful when you know how the other person is measuring "success."

Make a business case using the above benefits, and any others unique to your situation. This will help the hiring manager understand what's in it for them to spend the time. I avoid saying things like "This will help me…" (There is more information on the power of your language choices later.)

The short reason to avoid this kind of statement is because it subtly gives the impression that all recruiting is really the sole responsibility of the recruiter. It implies they are doing you a big favor by **helping you do your job.** That's not the impression that will create a partnership relationship.

Focus on things that are for the hiring manager's benefit—everything should be geared to answer the question they are silently asking themselves: "What's in it for me to spend the time?"

They will ask how much time you need. Don't try to squeeze yourself here. If it's a new kind of position or the first time you've done this kind of questioning with a hiring manager, look them in the eye (or sit up straight so your voice is clear and confident on the phone) and say "It will take **us** (notice a partnership assumption) about 45 minutes."

Don't say "I need about 45 minutes". Talking about what you "need" takes this out of a partnership relationship mental structure for the hiring manager. If you "need," then at a subtle level it implies they are doing you a favor.

This is their responsibility—we don't have to say that, of course. I just want you to remember it if it feels like they are pushing back. Stay calm and confident. Don't try to talk them into it by talking about what you "need." That's not how to build a business partner relationship.

If they say they can only spend 30 minutes, take it! Remember the hiring manager I told you about who went on and on after being asked about what was near and dear to him. If the time is still short, ask the most important questions—those critical to getting the search launched. You can ask the other questions as the process moves forward.

So congratulations! You got the meeting. In the next few techniques we'll talk about the magic questions. They will get you the information you need to increase the potential for a successful search. But even more fun, at the same time, they will advance your trusted advisor image to the hiring manager.

# Technique 6: How to Get the Whole Scoop Up Front

*"I have to tell you- that was the best intake meeting I have ever had. The **hiring manager said she was thoroughly impressed with the process**, the level of detail I was digging into, and that this was the most in-depth discussion she had had to date about a position when hiring for it. From this particular manager, especially, this was a huge compliment. So thank you! Your insight and guidance has been amazing."*

**HB., Senior Recruiter, Media Technology**

First, let's talk about a process you may be using already. This process is known by several different names, including Intake Form, Service Level Agreement or Partnership Level Agreement.

I've included a copy of the Comprehensive Launch document we used to launch our searches. I've shared this with many recruiters who tell me it has made a world of difference in their relationships with the hiring managers and their recruiting results. Not only do they get really good information to help their recruiting, but hiring managers are often blown away with this deep dive into their positions.

I don't know that the concept of service level or partnership level agreements ever really caught on nor if it was ever particularly effective. It was a good idea, but I never saw it make much difference when companies told me that's what they were using. Perhaps because the "commitments" and "agreements" were not really negotiated.

They were set by whoever designed the recruiting process. Then they were usually announced to the hiring manager, as in "I'll get back to you in 48 hours. Will you do the same?" or something similar.

Problem is that it's easy to say "yes" to that request without really thinking about it. So even in companies using this form of launch document, recruiters tell me one of their biggest issues (and time waster) was trying to get hiring managers to get back to them.

We'll talk about how to get hiring managers to make commitments they are more likely to keep. But for now we can probably agree that just telling them when to get back to us is a mega-exercise in futility.

Back to the Comprehensive Launch Document. Let's talk about it in two sections—one focusing on the position-specific information and one focusing on setting expectations and making commitments for both you and the hiring manager.

Unless you are in one of those "just post the job description" environments, you have probably had to create a job posting without much information other than the job description. So you know how hard it is to accurately convey what the job is and define what skills and experience will be necessary to do the job. And you're the expert.

Imagine how difficult it is for a hiring manager to sit down and fill in those blanks. They cannot always do it, but you can help them by guiding them through the necessary thought process.

Recruiters often lament that hiring managers don't know what they want. Probably true in more cases than we realize. I must admit that it has taken me an embarrassingly long time to realize what is probably a basic truth: Just because they have the word "hiring" in their titles doesn't necessarily mean they know everything they should about "hiring".

So let's help the hiring manager. It's in the best interest of a quality search and goes a long way to ensuring a happy hiring manager at the end. And the best part for you and me? We are now happy campers feeling great about our results and our relationship with the hiring manager.

The technique is all about the secret of asking questions. The Comprehensive Launch Document has the major questions you can ask to help the hiring manager think about many aspects of the position, the person, the success factors, the challenges, and more. A copy of this magic form is included in the forms section at the back of this document.

The benefits with these business-oriented questions, include:

- You'll be able to continue to build your business partner relationship
- You will get loads of information about the position, the requirements, etc.
- You will get a chance to hear how the hiring manager is selling their position.
- You'll get a chance to hear how the hiring manager sees themselves as a manager.
- You'll hear the key questions the hiring manager wants answered when you present or send them a candidate.
- You will get to hear your hiring manager's expectations and definition of what constitutes a success search.
- You and the hiring manager will get to make commitments to meet each other's expectations.

This form will also help you deal with or even avoid the following situations:

- Your hiring manager changes their mind about what they are looking for in the middle of your recruiting for the position without telling you.
- You keep submitting resumes and candidates and the hiring manager wants to see more…and more…and more.
- You cannot get the hiring manager to tell you exactly what is wrong with the resumes and candidates they are rejecting.

Think about how many questions on the hiring manager satisfaction survey from Technique 3 will be addressed with this information. **Once you know how someone defines satisfaction, it's much easier to achieve success with them**. And if it turns out their expectations are unrealistic, you can start the dialog you must have to share realities of the candidate market place and come up with a new definition.

*We recently had a client who had a version of this form already in use. We were impressed. Until we learned how the form got filled out. The recruiter would send a blank form to the hiring manager when a new requisition was received. The hiring manager was supposed to complete the form and send it back to the recruiter. The recruiter would fill out their section and email the finalized form to the hiring manager. Where is the relationship building in that?*

*So most of the benefits inherent in the use of this form were, as they say, lost in translation.*

*And then the best part of the story. We did ask for a meeting with the hiring manager "to fill in some of the blanks." When we started to discuss the information that he had put on the form, he got a puzzled look on his face. "Where are you getting that from?" he asked. When we showed him the form that the recruiting team had given us, he realized that the information was incorrect.*

*He was somewhat embarrassed to admit that he never filled out the forms himself. He had his administrative assistant do it. And because she was not familiar with the various job descriptions, she had inadvertently used information from a very old job description. It was outdated and inaccurate.*

*Imagine if the recruiter had just taken the form as he got it from the hiring manager and launched his efforts to find people who fit that job description! There is no way the hiring manager would have been a satisfied internal customer at the end of that experience.*

You can ask the questions in whatever order makes sense to you based on what is important to know and the amount of time the hiring manager has scheduled for you (a minimum of 30 minutes, I hope!). In the earlier example we engaged the hiring manager in the process by asking about his business first. Then he was willing to spend time on the other questions.

There may be times when you omit some of the questions just because they aren't applicable to the position you're discussing or because of time constraints. It's perfectly fine to set a priority ranking for your questions. Sometimes you may know the answer.

But for those really important questions, I always like to check my understanding with the hiring manager.

Be sure to check out **Bonus Report 2 How to Have Your Best Launch Ever** for more tools!

Sometimes hiring managers will not or cannot give you the answer you need. Try asking the question another way. If it becomes clear to you the manager hasn't even thought about the question before you asked it and is struggling to come up with a good answer, you may want to back off for now. I try to avoid making the manager feel inept because they haven't thought about the things I'm asking.

Hiring managers often don't consider, as surprising as it may be, is what they want the new person to accomplish in the first 6 or 12 months. It's certainly critical if the new person is to be considered successful to have these things defined, but usually not critical to your conducting a successful search.

So if it's clear the manager is a little embarrassed that they cannot easily recite those goals, I let them know it's ok not to have them at this time. However, that said, if you can get that information and include it in your posting, candidates will be very appreciative to be able to see what they will be expected to accomplish and the timeframe for doing those things.

**Want to know how to endear yourself to every hiring manager?**

Many times hiring managers think recruiters are not willing to look for candidates with ALL the qualities the hiring manager wants. Well, there are valid reasons for that of course—more about that later.

But for now, ask the hiring manager to tell you **everything** they would like candidates to have.

When we tell hiring managers to ask for everything up front—they will love it. Maybe no one has ever encouraged them to "Ask for everything." It will really get them thinking. They will tell you things they wouldn't have if you hadn't given them permission to ask for it all.

In the past, the hiring manager may have been told they were looking for too much in one candidate. So they aren't telling you everything they would really like to have, but trust me—they interview for all those things! They want more but aren't telling you. Of course what can happen is, as you send them candidates, they are really looking for something they haven't even told you about.

So I always say, "Tell me everything you would like to have. Go for it. Then we'll see what exists in the marketplace." (NOTICE I didn't promise they would get everything--just that we would see if their dream candidate actually exists.)

This actually gives you more credibility as a recruiter because you're going to see what exists in the marketplace. The hiring manager won't feel you are pushing back and won't wonder if perhaps they could have had everything if you had just been willing to look for it.

Of course, we all know that isn't true. But perception is critical, so be sure to influence it with this approach.

You may hear things you didn't expect. You almost always will hear good recruiting information that goes far beyond the job description.

So you will have more of those ideal candidates show up, simply because you're able to be on the look out for them. Hard to find something when you aren't really sure what it is. Everyone wins!

Now on to the magic questions. They will get you great information to help you attract and land the ideal candidates. Plus, asking them will clearly demonstrate your value-add and expertise.

# Technique 7: The Magic Questions to Get Critical Details

In this technique, we'll discuss some of the essential questions you must ask your hiring manager. If you want to build a consultative recruiter reputation as fast as possible, questions—including the ones here—are the fastest way to do that. And you get two bonuses with these great questions:

1. You get essential information that helps you get more of the great candidates and close the req faster.
2. You build a trust business partnership relationship with your hiring manager. You'll be amazed and delighted when you realize they see you in a very different light—all due to a few fabulous questions.

If you are in a "just post the job description" environment, it may take some courage to tell hiring managers you want to do a launch meeting before posting anything. And you may as well tell them that posting a job description is not the best way to get the best candidates interested and thus close their req as quickly as possible.

Maybe the job descriptions in your company are different, but I have never seen a job description that I felt gave me the critical information. So if your job descriptions raise lots of questions, use the Comprehensive Launch Document at the end of this ebook. You'll be amazed at what you learn!

Everyone has an internal answer to these questions. Until they are asked, however, they probably don't share that information with you. It always raises eyebrows and brings "ah-ha's" when that information is heard out loud for the first time.

Here are just a few of the great benefits you and the hiring manager will get from this discussion.

- You'll hear the key questions the hiring manager wants answered when you present or send them a candidate. This section alone will save you time and effort. At this point, don't be surprised if you hear for the first time about something that is really important to the hiring manager.

  Just as importantly, it will give you a common ground to discuss the candidates. Read the story coming up about a time when we did NOT do this, and the mess it created!

- You will get to hear your hiring manager's expectations about the number and timing of seeing candidates. If those expectations are realistic, that's great. However, there is a teeny tiny possibility they won't be—right?

  This will be the place to have that all important discussion about what is realistic. Technique 9 will give you some good ways to have that kind of discussion. It's critical to have it at this point. Don't get nervous that you'll have to give the hiring manager bad news—we'll look at how to do that and even strengthen your relationship at the same time.

- You will get to hear what all those vague terms in the job description really mean. The elephant in the room about job descriptions is that when someone reads them, they may think they know what the job is. But have the courage to ask what specific terms mean and you may be in for a surprise. I've had hiring managers be surprised at what was in the job description, say they are not sure what a particular phrase was supposed to mean, and/or decide it doesn't belong in that job description. I've seen job descriptions put together by a committee that actually ended up being three separate jobs!

PLEASE: Don't ever take a job description at face value. I know it may seem like it makes sense, but it won't ever make a good posting. When you're ready, I have lots of helpful and specific information in this area for you. Just visit:
**Bonus Report #3: Creating Irresistible Job Postings**

Often hiring managers say success is "quality candidates quickly." So what are they thinking when they say quickly? Let's have an honest discussion around exactly what they want, what they need, what the challenges might be to meeting that timeline, etc. You understand the challenges external conditions such as time of year, the economy, your geographic location, etc., may present to the search. It's always good to talk about them with the hiring manager. They may not have thought of all those constraints.

This is also a time you can discuss what *a quality candidate* means to them—how do they define that? I ask the question just like that.

What is the reason to ask that question?

1. They may not have a clear definition of quality—meaning they really aren't totally sure what they are looking for in a candidate. Thus they may not know it when they see it. And how can you give them quality when they aren't sure what it is? It critical to have that discussion **now** rather than weeks into the search! Hiring managers who aren't sure how they have defined *quality* are going to say things like "I'll know it when I see it." "Just didn't see the candidate as a fit." And the ever popular "Just send me some more candidates."

2. Their definition of quality may be something they haven't even told you until this point.

   *I remember a hiring manager who defined quality, when I asked her, as someone with whom she didn't have to worry about what they were doing on a Thursday afternoon. Clearly a unique definition! But a key piece of information for our search was to understand what that meant. What did she mean by that?*

   *We also wanted to understand how she would know she was meeting a candidate for whom that would be true— what would be her evidence that a candidate fit her unique definition of quality?*

   That information became a key piece of our screening process. I believe the reason we closed that search so quickly was because we had finally heard that critical piece of information. And no less importantly, we had talked to her about something that no recruiter had ever elicited from her. That's consultative recruiting at its most fun!

How you manage the hiring manager's answers will help you go further in creating a business partner relationship. Technique 9 will give you some suggestions of subtle changes to the way you say things--little changes that get amazingly big results.

Here is an example, though you probably have a lot of your own examples, of the cost of not getting critical information up front.

*It was a time that I went against my better judgment and did the **Ok, Go Away Get Away**. You may have done that yourself. I let the corporate recruiting manager talk me out of having the very meeting I'm saying you need to have. I was trying to help her save* *face with her hiring managers because they thought she had been working on the positions for the last 3 weeks. The truth was that she hadn't even posted the positions because she was so busy.*

*The predictable result was that it made for a rocky start, some wasted time, and most difficult for us, made us look like we were not business partners to the hiring managers.*

*We were recently engaged by the corporate recruiter at a large consumer products company to assist with some searches. They had a great brand and had many responses to their postings. They just didn't have the time to contact those applicants, screen them and bring the great ones forward to the hiring managers.*

*The recruiting team at the client was puzzled about why candidates they thought should be a fit were rejected by the hiring manager after they interviewed. That should have been my signal that a meeting with the hiring manager was absolutely called for.*

*We screened candidates according to the questions the hiring manager had requested. The recruiting team just wanted us to use those questions and did not want us to take the hiring manager's time for an upfront meeting.*

*So we were stunned when the first candidate we presented washed out during the interview with the hiring manager. When we got the hiring manager to talk about where the candidate did not measure up, we realized that the screening questions we had were all wrong—**all of them were wrong**. We worked with the hiring manager to redo the questions, and finally we were all on the same page.*

*An upfront meeting would have saved a lot of time and been easier on all of us, including the hiring manager and the candidates!*

OK, lesson learned—again!

The next technique is one of my favs and will save you tons of time and energy trying to track down your hiring managers to give you feedback. You may want to try this one first!

It works every time, even the first time. And no one is going to mistake you for an order taker again when you start using this.

# Technique 8: How to Get Commitments and What to Do When They Aren't Met

**Woops. The hiring manager didn't keep their commitment. Now you have to start the chase all over again.**

Be sure to check out the Strategy Techniques #1 which has the detailed approach to finally getting hiring managers to give you feedback!

Recruiters just seem to naturally play nice with others, want to make life easier for their hiring managers, like being helpful, etc. All great goals. So how do you behave in ways that are comfortable for you, yet help you get your job done?

Of course there are those times when the recruiter is so frustrated they act in ways that can damage their business partner image. Any time I've met a recruiter who is out on the ledge because of something their hiring manager has done, I can totally understand their feelings.

At the same time, I've often seen that when we get to this level of frustration, we don't always have the ***ability*** to have the best conversations. It's possible to blow your image as a business partner very easily at this point.

Let's discuss a way to get hiring managers to meet their commitments while you build your business partner image at the same time. It may seem a little counter-intuitive, but try it. Here is an example.

*We were working with a hiring manager at a large national company, and he truly had a busy schedule—one of those where he went from meeting to meeting. When we had the conference call to launch the search using the Comprehensive Launch approach, we explained that we would want to talk to him at least once a week. We explained what the reason was for the weekly calls—so we could present the new candidates, get his feedback about the candidate he had met that week, and to set the strategy for the next week—all things that would move the search quickly. (I like to explain to the hiring manager what is in it for them to agree to any commitment I ask for.)*

*He agreed that he would make himself available for a weekly meeting. We asked what would be the best way to schedule those meetings, and he responded that his admin managed his calendar. Okey dokey, looks like a commitment, sounds like a commitment, etc., etc.*

*We quickly saw that while his admin did **try** to manage his calendar, he constantly put in meetings over the meetings she scheduled for him. It took nearly two weeks to get the first meeting scheduled, and we wasted a lot of our time trying to get it set up, and frustrated the candidates who were hoping for quick decisions about whether they would be interviewed. Sound familiar? What to do to get us back on tract?*

*We finally got the call set up. On the call, we went through all the items on the agenda. And then asked him: "It really seems like the process we discussed to schedule these weekly calls isn't working for you. What would work better for you?"*

*And then we stopped talking and waited. He came up with the solution, which was to schedule the next four calls in advance—and we did that while we were on the phone with him.*

I love this approach of asking and then not saying anything until they answer, as we discussed earlier. It's a key concept in the psychology of creating business partnerships. I call it the "Yippee, I don't have to have all the answers or solutions" concept.

You can drive yourself crazy trying to come up with solutions that will work for your hiring managers. Or you can just pose the question and let them come up with what will work for them.

Easier on you, and easier for them to commit to their own suggestion.

## The Two-Step Process to get Commitment

Good news: I have this on a one-page doc at the end of this ebook so you can print it out and keep it close to you. It truly works—the first time and every time. It's called: Give Me A Commitment.

It's certainly not unusual to have had hiring managers who do not respond to us on a timely basis. It takes multiple follow up emails, calls, etc. All that follow-up time is adding to the "time to fill" computation, plus wasting so much time that could be spent finding candidates.

So here is an easy, non-confrontational way to get hiring managers to not only commit but to keep their commitments. It's just 2 simple steps that you just keep doing until you and the hiring manager are happily committed.

## Step 1: Let them commit:

Ask for a commitment as early as possible in the process—ideally when you start the search. But this technique works at any point you need it. For example, let's say you want to get a commitment regarding how quickly they will get back to you with feedback on resumes you've sent them.

Here's an example of how to ask for that commitment:

"When I send a resume for you to review, how soon do you think you'll be able to get your feedback to me?"

Now the critical part: **Stop talking at this point**. I know it's tempting to give them options, alternatives, offer to keep tracking them down, etc., but don't. Let them think it through and come up with their own timetable.

If they ask about what would be best, you could say something like " 24 hours would be the best way to keep the search moving quickly. How does that work for you?". Or some version of that. But let the decision be theirs.

Now you can proceed as if you fully trust they will keep that commitment because they just might.

But in case they don't, see step 2.

## Step 2: When they don't keep their original commitment:

So you sent resumes and guess what? The hiring manager didn't keep their commitment about how quickly they would get back to you with feedback.

So now you say (preferably in a meeting or at least on the phone, not email) "When we spoke earlier, you thought that it would work for you to get your thoughts on the resumes to me in (state their original commitment). That doesn't seem to work for you. What would be a better timeframe for you to provide feedback?"

It's important your tone is one of truly wanting to get a commitment that works for both of you, and not be trying to point out their "failure to keep a commitment."

Now the critical part: **Stop talking at this point**....you know the rest.

Lather, rinse, repeat. It's a great step to strengthen your business partnership with your hiring managers. And over time you will be spending less and less time trying to track them down to get feedback, find out what they like and don't like in candidates they have interviewed, and even if you should keep recruiting to find more candidates.

Now what if they give you a timeline that is totally unacceptable. I've never had this happen but I surely know it could. Here's the technique that will get things back on track.

Let's say the hiring manager says it will be a week after they interview a candidate before they will get back to you. Rather a long (and unacceptable) time frame.

So you say,

> "Well, if that's what works for you, let's make that work for the search. Your feedback is important to me so I know if I'm moving in the right direction, bringing you the right candidates, etc. So to avoid going in the wrong direction and wasting everyone's time, I'll just put your search on soft pause until I get feedback from you If someone great shows up, I'll absolutely screen and present them to you. But otherwise I'll just be on a soft pause until I get your feedback."

Remember, all of this is on the Give Me A Commitment cheat sheet in the Appendix at the back.

**Uh oh, you cannot keep a commitment (Admit it—it happens no matter how hard you try.)**

Now the equally important discussion of how to approach the hiring manager when you cannot keep your commitment. I've found an essential element here is your attitude—how you feel about the fact you have to reset a commitment. If you see it as a failure on your part, what is conveyed to your hiring manager? That you failed at something. We didn't make the hiring manager feel like a failure because they missed keeping a commitment. I don't want you to feel that way either.

I've provided a worksheet called **Delivering Bad News** in the Appendix that will guide you through the key steps.

First, don't think of it as a crisis. It's not a personal indictment of your ability. I define crisis as a life or death situation. This isn't one of those, so it is just a situation to be managed.

Let your hiring manager know as early as possible that there is the possibility the commitment will not be met. That communication goes a long way to creating a relationship of trust.

I've seen recruiters (and you probably have also) who don't let hiring managers know they won't have candidates by the end of the week as promised. They "hope" someone will turn up. Hope is a nice component of a strategy, but if it's all you've got, you may want to rethink. It's always best to give bad news while there is still time to regroup.

Explain what happened (briefly). One thing to remember is that the hiring manager may not care a lot about why you cannot make the commitment or deadline. Please be brief here. People are busy and don't always need the details. As recruiters we're trained to focus on and interpret the details. Remember the hiring manager may not love the details as much as you do. And sometimes too much detail can be viewed as an excuse. Avoid avoid avoid.

Lay out your new strategy: If you have some thoughts on what needs to change in your go-forward strategy, share them with the hiring manager. If the strategy requires the hiring manager to make some changes, it's a good time to share what you think needs to happen. Ask if they would be "open" to trying some new things.

Make a new commitment. Get the hiring manager's commitment as well, if appropriate.

### The One Thing You Might Consider Never Saying When You Miss a Commitment

The one statement that I think undercuts your business partner relationship is "I'm doing everything I **can**." This always leaves people with a subtle feeling that maybe there is something else you could or should be doing—if you were just more capable, competent, whatever. It also can come across as whiny, no matter what tone you use.

You'll hear this "I'm doing everything I can …" statement a lot. Notice how often it leaves you wondering if there is something else that could be done and it isn't being done because the person doesn't know to do it.

It doesn't inspire confidence. And it sometimes sounds inept.

A much more confident statement is "I'm doing everything possible to…"

This means you've thought of and done EVERYTHING that could be possible be done. You are the expert on this. Try making that change; I think it can absolutely change how others view your ability.

The next technique will help you even more with new ways to talk to your hiring managers to strengthen your image as the recruiting expert while it also builds your relationship with them.

# Technique 9: How You Say It Makes All the Difference

Here are more subtle changes in your language that will change your relationship and image, and they won't even know what you're doing differently. You'll love the results.

One of the skills that makes recruiters successful can also make it difficult for them to build business partner relationships. Recruiters like people and are really nice people themselves. I don't mean to imply that recruiters are just order takers. However, in my thirteen years of recruiting experience, I've seen them treated like that—a lot!!

Here are some examples of how simple changes in your words will get you what you need while even building your relationship and image as a trusted advisor.

Conversation can be like a chess game. You'll be most successful when you think ahead. We're not trying to be manipulative here but simply to be able to have a conversation where a) you're viewed as a business partner, b) you make your point in a way it can be heard and c) everyone wins.

Here are some phrases we probably all use, and some new ones I'd like you to try out.

**Help me.**

This can be very useful but only in a limited set of circumstances. When we ask for help, the person who "helps" you believes they are actually doing a part of your job for you. Think about it. They probably won't say it out loud, but there it is.

I like to do the "help me" when I want someone to explain something to me. This is clearly a situation—and I'm happy to admit it—where I don't know something. People are usually very pleased to be asked to share their knowledge.

I've always found that people like people who ask their advice or opinion. You have to be honest when you ask, and you must listen to the answer.

**I'm confused and/or I'm wondering**

I use one or both of these when I want to have a discussion to come up with a new conclusion. For example, those situations you've undoubtedly experienced where the hiring manager is saying conflicting things about what they are looking for, etc. These are a great place to use this communication style.

*I got a chance to use it a lot when we were working with a large bio-medical device company to fill sales executive positions around the country. It was a highly professional, classy organization but the hiring managers were initially very opposed to working with us. They all had their own ways of doing things and were not planning to change them!*

*To attract the kinds of candidates they wanted, they determined that a key element of their branding was the speed with which they made decisions, brought new products to market, solved customer issues, etc.*

*We had a fabulous candidate who had already interviewed with all the key decision makers. Everyone agreed this candidate would be a great addition to the sales team in the Southeast. Everyone, including the candidate, thought the interview process was over.*

*Then, when we all thought we were going to offer stage, the hiring manager decided to have more people interview the candidate. Talk about a really really really bad candidate experience! And this hiring manager, especially, had been very vocal about his strong objection to having to work with us.*

*So I said "I'm confused." I knew if I went head to head with the hiring manager, all I would succeed in doing would be to get him to dig his heels in about his new plan.*

*"I'm confused" certainly aren't fighting words. They won't imply a battle is about to start. They seem to ask the listener to explain something to you. People will listen to your next words when you start with these words.*

*So I said, "I'm confused about the message you want to give the candidate. We've all agreed that speed was one of your key differentiators, did I get that correct?" (Tone and intention are critical here. You must be in an inquisitive mode. If you're just trying to prove the manager is wrong, that comes out in your tone and usually doesn't get you where you want to go.)*

*The hiring manager agreed—without my having to ask him if he remembered that we had all made that decision.*

*So, again in my "I'm confused" tone, I asked "I'm wondering if this new round of interviews will support that brand we've been working to create in the marketplace. I can tell you believe it's important to have more people talk to the candidate. More interviews may not be in keeping with the speed differentiator. So, in this case, which do you feel is more important?"*

*I was going to let the hiring manager make the decision; I really trust them--almost all the time. But I wanted to put the information out there in a way that would help him see the potential consequences. And I wanted to do it in as non-confrontational way as possible.*

*So if he were to change his mind, he could do it in a very face-saving way. It would almost be as if he were clearing up MY confusion by making a different decision. In this case, however, the hiring manager did NOT decide to change his plan to have the candidate run the interview gauntlet again.*

*What was the outcome? Bless his heart, the candidate was willing to keep moving through the process, and was eventually hired.*

*The hiring manager (and everyone else involved) realized that the whole decision to interview and interview was really driven by the manager's antagonism to us and our candidates. But because we didn't confront and embarrass him during that childish power play, he became one of our biggest supporters.*

So when you're willing to ask what could be considered a silly question, you will get new information as you are building a business relationship.

### I can't find—a NO NO statement

Many recruiters tell the hiring manager they "will find" or "cannot find" the right candidates at some point in the search. By now you probably can identify what that implies: you aren't doing your job or you cannot do your job.

Of course you and I know that's not what you meant. The fact there are not enough candidates with the requisite requirements doesn't mean you cannot or have not done your job. Not having enough candidates can be the result of a million different things, including:

- They are rare in the marketplace.
- The message and brand of your company aren't sufficient to draw them out to apply for your position.
- The compensation the manager wants to pay is way under the going market rate.

So to have this conversation with the hiring manager, it's important to remember the situation is a result of the marketplace. If candidates with all the requirements at the salary range you were given don't exist, there isn't any way to "find" them.

So let the hiring manager know "there are very few people in the market who have the qualifications at the salary range you are thinking to pay". Use "market feedback" to talk about potential issues with the company reputation that may be hindering your search. Give the hiring manager some facts based on your "research." This can be information from other searches, the conversations you're having with potential candidates, etc.

This can be a tough change to make. When we can say we "found" the candidate, there is a lot of satisfaction in that success. The downside is that not being able to "find" the candidate can create a perception that the issue is the recruiter, not any one of the nine million other reasons the candidate isn't showing up.

It's a challenge to have this both ways. Try this approach and see it works. It will be subtle but it will make a difference.

*I had been engaged to do a search for the new CEO of a large US non-profit organization, and was doing the launch meeting with the Board of Directors. Believe me, it was tempting to say I would "find" great candidates. It feels good to attribute that part of the search success to me.*

*I had to keep reminding myself that keeping the focus on the marketplace was the best approach. I certainly talked about my strategy to locate the best candidates and screen them appropriately so the Board would see only the best. But I kept reiterating that the success of the search would depend on what the marketplace of candidates felt about the opportunity and what candidates raised their hand to be considered.*

That really is what determines a lot of search success, and it is important to reinforce that with your hiring managers.

### Ask Rather than State Your Request

Many times we say things like "Just give me a call if you need to change the interview schedule", or "After the interview, please let me know what you think about the candidate." And find out that whatever we were hoping for doesn't happen.

Here's a simple change that will increase your odds of getting that call (or anything else you need the hiring manager to do). Do this instead and it will remind you of the **Give Me A Commitment** approach.

"Will you please let me know if you need to change the schedule?"

**DO NOT SAY ANOTHER WORD** until they respond.

The hiring manager has now made a verbal commitment to you. It turns out that this approach generates a stronger commitment level than the first one of just making a statement and getting agreement.

**How To Avoid Going Out On the "That Won't Work." Limb**

No matter how strong my relationships are, rarely tell them "that won't work". If I'm right, then I've visibly made the other person wrong. Most of us don't like to be wrong, even less do we like to be made wrong in front of anyone else.

Secondly, I might be the one who is wrong. No matter how experienced, smart, thoughtful we are, there are many instances where our predictions just might be wrong. We are dealing with people, after all, and people aren't always predictable.

Instead of the "won't work" statement, I use one of the statements we discussed above. Almost any of them will help you give the hiring manager a gentle reminder of the issues without either of you having to be on the receiving end of an "I told you so."

No big deal if you're wrong about something, but you can mitigate the impact that can have on your image as a recruiting consultant by taking a gentler approach to the conversation. So for example, rather than say "You'll never find a candidate who meets your requirements for the salary you are offering," I say "Let's see what the marketplace tells us."

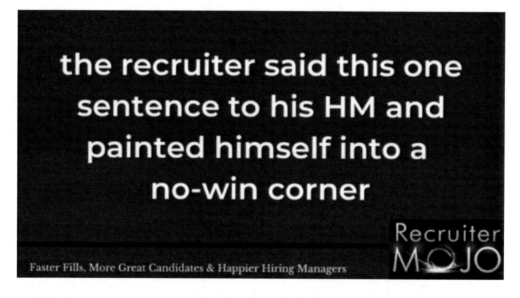

*Eric had 12 years of recruiting experience and had been recruiting for a niche technology firm for 3 years. While he was filling tough positions, he was very frustrated with his hiring managers. He felt they didn't believe him about the challenges of landing the candidates they wanted.*

*As we discussed those challenges, I felt that Eric had very validate points.*

*Eric gave me an example from a recent search. The hiring manager wanted to fill a position in a very competitive technology. Those candidates in these technologies tended to be in a few Northern California areas which would have been prime areas for sourcing.*

*Unfortunately, the hiring manager wanted that person to be located in Southern California. All the makings of a tough long search with lots of opportunity for friction between Eric and the hiring manager.*

*But Eric had made matters much worse when he told the hiring manager, "You won't find anyone at your salary who is in Southern California or willing to move there."*

*Now Eric had painted himself into a corner. What was he going to say to the hiring manager when candidates showed up who were at the salary and were located in Southern CA?*

*Because of course those candidates did show up. There weren't a lot but enough to a) fill the position and b) prove Eric wrong.*

*Now does he show the results of his good recruiting and admit he was wrong? Does he look for candidates in Northern California only in order to prove his point?*

*He's really in a bind on this one. Of course he did present the So. Cal candidates and the position was filled. But Eric recognizes how this one sentence really damaged his credibility.*

*The next section gave Eric lots of options for the future, because I'm sure his challenges will remain. But they will be recruiting challenges, not hiring manager challenges with this approach.*

## When they are unrealistic

Here is a place I do NOT to tell a hiring manager they are wrong. They can be unrealistic about a whole host of things—as you certainly know. I make an agreement with the hiring manager "to go to market" with their requirements.

Then in a week or as soon as I'll have some information, I promise to get back to them to let them know how the available candidates fit their requirements.

Remember, this is a situation of what the market looks like, not of your ability to "find" these non-existent candidates.

See Technique 13 for details on this conversation. I've needed to use it a lot!!

## And one last example of thinking about how your words influence your relationships and how people perceive you

Here's a quick example of how changing the way you say things will change your relationship.

*We wrote a marketing- and candidate-centric posting as a part of our engagement with a client to find their new SVP Sales. The hiring manager made a lot of changes, some quite helpful and some that seemed less so. But since those changes didn't jeopardize the marketing message of the specification, we went with them.*

*In acknowledging that we got the changes and appreciated his input, the recruiter drafted an email that said:*

**"Thank you for your comments, this helps me get a better understanding of the position and the areas that we need to focus on."**

*This **wording implies**: we didn't have a sufficient understanding of the position nor of the key areas of experience the candidates needed to have.*

*Since we had spent nearly two hours in a launch meeting with this hiring manager to get exactly that information, it probably was not wise to give him the impression that we still hadn't gotten it by the time we left!*

*A simple change takes the focus off implying that we weren't sufficiently informed about the position. A better focus is to let the hiring manager know he had made a useful contribution to the marketing for his position.*

*Here is one suggestion on a different message to the hiring manager: "**Thank you for your comments; they are really helpful in creating a compelling marketing message for your ideal candidates.**"*

*So he feels good about what he did, and we look much more professional and prepared. At least in my opinion.*

## Bold Questions

It's always interesting to ask these questions at the end of any information-gathering meeting. Often, perhaps not always, but often, you will hear something critical and brand new.

What question should I have asked you? What question do you wish I had asked?

## A Counter-Intuitive Strategy to Get Change

Sometimes you have to let something happen contrary to your preference in order to get your point across—and get the necessary changes made.

Do these techniques work every time?

The interesting thing is that even when they don't work right away, this approach will advance your business partner image—and your credibility. And ultimately you will end up with things the way the way you want them to be—without having to be confrontational.

In a confrontation, usually there is a winner and a loser. Even if you win the battle, your relationship with a hiring manager will need repair.

Here's what happened with that Sales Executive search I told you about earlier with the large medical device company. *The hiring manager decided to go ahead with the new expanded interview schedule. The candidate made it through the additional interviews and did get an offer, which he accepted. (Good thing I didn't tell the hiring manager he was wrong and predict that the candidate would back out if he had to do more interviews! That would have ended my credibility with him. That's why I carefully pick where I made predictions of dire consequences—I could be wrong!)*

*At the same time, the people in the expanded interview process felt they had not treated the candidate in accordance with their brand of speed. In truth, they also resented the fact they had to interview and re-interview the candidate.*

*Word of that got back to the hiring manager. Smart man that he was, he realized I had tried to save him from this bad press. I never had to say, "I told you so." Now the hiring manager and I had a new relationship from then on. He started to really talk to me about search strategy, what his plans were, and how to get a good hire while creating a good candidate experience. We were finally really working together.*

So those phrases can be helpful ways to state your case without having to challenge directly. There are times to take a stand, of course. But always try to have these kinds of conversations first.

Questions that start with any of the following are more likely to elicit a thoughtful exchange of ideas and strengthen your relationship:

"Would you be open to…"

"What are your thoughts about…"

"Would you mind if…"

"What do you think the impact would be if we…"

Now that we've got a commitment to give you feedback, that's one challenge down. But now we have to get feedback that tells us something.

Technique 10 sets out how you help your hiring manager give key information. This helps that frustrating situation where the search goes on and on because no one is sure what the hiring manager is thinking. Often including the hiring manager!

# Technique 10: How To Get Feedback That Tells You Something.

"Send more resumes. I'll-know-it-when-I-see-it paralysis."

"Not a fit. Can't tell you why. I've just got a gut feeling."

"I haven't seen enough candidates."

In addition to these wasting a lot of your time and creating a lot of frustration for you, they impact your metrics such as "time to fill" and "conversion ratio."

And of course there is the impact on for the candidates.

It's difficult (more like impossible, actually) to create a strategy with this kind of non-information. So recruiters are often left in a position of simply having to provide more resumes—and more—and more.

---

*I think one of the reasons hiring managers say these things is that they cannot articulate either what they are looking for or why someone isn't a fit.*

---

Earlier I mentioned how long it took me to figure out that just because they had the title "hiring" manager, that didn't mean they really knew how to hire—or that they were confident of their abilities to identify what skills a position required and what skills a candidate had.

One of the really great outcomes from using the Comprehensive Launch document is all the information you will be able to gather in that discussion. This alone may help hiring managers really think about what they are looking for. It certainly gives you some information so you can have a data-rich conversation about a resume and/or candidate.

If your hiring manager does not like the resumes or candidates you're sending, ask for a time when you can review them together in the context of what the manager has already told you about what they are looking for. During the launch conversation, the two of you discussed all the elements of the position, the experience and skills the candidates should have, etc.

Now that the hiring manager has seen some resumes or candidates, have any of those requirements perhaps changed? Sometimes when hiring managers start seeing resumes, they realize they want to add, subtract or modify their earlier statements about what is required.

To help the manager feel comfortable about changing their mind, I give them an *out* during the launch conversation. I tell them when I expect to have the first batch of resumes or candidates. Sometimes it's just one or two, sometimes a few more. Those are "calibration candidates." That means those are the ones where we make sure the requirements have been defined, and we've sent resumes that are on target.

I tell hiring managers that when they can see actual candidate resumes, it makes it easier for them to truly calibrate what they want. I also let them know we'll have that conversation after the manager has seen those calibration resumes early in the process, so I don't spend time going down a path we later decide isn't quite right.

Depending on the job you're seeking to fill and the candidate pool for that job, I like to set expectations about how many resumes or candidates the hiring manager is going to see in that first round, and when I anticipate having them to the manager. Of course, that all depends on the particular job you're filling, etc., so modify this approach to fit your situation.

That approach sets expectations that

a) we will discuss resumes/candidates early in the search process and,

b) those resumes will provide a model for future resumes.

If there are going to be changes in the requirements, let's hear them as early in the process as possible. In fact, let's use this strategy to draw them out. And it's almost always easier for a hiring manager to do that when they are looking at actual resumes or have spoken to a candidate or two.

If they are still struggling to give you any details about their evaluation of the resumes or the candidates, ask them to spend a minute with you going over the original list of requirements, screening questions and desirable answers to as they relate to each resume or candidate. That sometimes is enough to get them on track, and you start to get information flowing from your hiring manager. This process will undoubtedly uncover some interesting perceptions and evaluations—on both sides.

Is it possible the hiring manager is giving you this non-responsive feedback because they don't feel they have the time to explain further? Hiring managers wear many hats, recruiting being only one of them. They almost always have very full plates. Most people will acknowledge that if they were to fill their open positions they might not be so busy. Still it's often a challenge to find the time to do what would make life better!

So if this could be the reason, ask the hiring manager how you can make the resume or candidate discussion with you easier. How about over a cup of coffee--everyone deserves a break now and then. Ask them what would work for them. If they come up with a solution, it's more likely to be a lasting solution that will work for both of you. Having to chase them for days or getting a "not interested in that candidate" response isn't a solution.

In fact, it's my experience and observation that frequent follow-up attempts are probably not creating a consultative recruiter image. Unfortunately, lots of calls, emails, etc., to continually request information probably relegate you to an order taker image, to say nothing of how much of your time gets wasted.

If you're still not getting the information you need, a frank conversation is a good next step. It's a "how can we make this work for you" exchange. If you loosely follow the Bad News Worksheet included in the documents at the end of this book, you'll be able to guide the hiring manager to finding a solution that will work for both of you.

### *One Recruiter's Story: How A Small Question Created A Real Business Partnership*

This is a great example of using multiple techniques to resolve a challenge and build your consultative recruiter image at the same time. In this instance, John stopped doing the *Ok, Go Away Get Away* and stayed to ask just one small question.

John is a great recruiter I was coaching who called in total frustration with one of his HMs. Perhaps you can relate!

*John was working on a req for which there were very few interested candidates. He had finally found a great one, but was blown away with his HM's response.*

*She was declining the as-perfect-as-we-going-to-get candidate because they are missing something not even on the requirements list—a college degree.*

*Sometimes these kinds of objections come at us from left field, and there would be no way to predict the HM would respond this way. And on the surface they don't seem to make any sense, just as this one doesn't.*

*How can the HM turn candidates down when they don't have something that wasn't even required in the first place? Aughhh!*

*In these situations, we are probably tempted, as John was, to point out to the HM how difficult it is to find candidates for the position, how lucky the HM is to have this candidate, etc. And he was right!*

*Unfortunately, that approach probably won't move your HM from their position even a little bit. Just telling them what they probably already know isn't new information and isn't compelling enough to change their mind. Remember, to tell won't sell.*

*In fact, if all you're going to do is one of these party-line type of conversation, don't bother. It will feel like push-back to your HM.*

*In a friendly "can I ask you a question" John said "How do you see a college degree will help the person in this position?"*

*You have to be careful it doesn't sound like your real question is "How can you be so ridiculous as to demand a college degree for this job that so clearly doesn't require it?"*

*What the hiring manager responded was totally unexpected. She said, "Well, actually I don't think it should be required. Unfortunately, my boss thinks it is an essential, and I cannot get him to change his mind. So we're stuck with that requirement."*

*John got his hiring manager to share something really important to her. Now he understands why she has been making the decisions that turned down his candidates. And he has moved into a much stronger relationship with her.*

*All because he avoided the "ok, go away get away" during a French Fry moment and asked one small question.*

## One last thing

Sometimes I've had hiring managers ask me a question that fell outside the information I had gathered about a candidate. So that is either a critical question I may need to add to the candidate screening protocol or it may just be idle curiosity.

When this happens, many recruiters say, "I don't know but I can get you that information." And often that means the discussion stops until the recruiter goes and gets the information, gives it to the hiring manager, the hiring manager reflects, and only then does the process restart.

I've found that the following question will prevent that stop-start delay in many cases. I say to the hiring manager, "I don't have that information but I can get it for you. Do you need that information before deciding if you want to move ahead?"

In almost every case, the hiring manager says "No, just wondering. Let's move ahead." Or "I'd like you to get the information but I can tell I would like to see this candidate."

Sometimes they will want the information before they can decide on next steps but that is more rare than you might think. I've always been amazed at how often the question was just "nice to know" but not critical to know in order to make a decision to move ahead. This one question alone has saved recruiters hours of delay.

So now let's talk about metrics—the ones that really matter.

Sometimes, metrics are used to try to improve recruiting results. But historical data doesn't always help understand what really happened, much less improve the future.

# Technique 11: Metrics s'metrics—How To Track What Really Matters To Those Who Really Matter

Just about everyone agrees that metrics are important. There is less agreement on how and what should be measured.

What companies actually do measure ranges from everything to nothing.

- Some do not track anything at all. In fact, some do not have any mechanism to track recruiting statistics.
- Some track a few traditional metrics like time to fill, cost to fill and average number of requisitions each recruiter carries.
- Some are tracking everything in detail. They have extensive spreadsheets with things such as how many calls are made by each recruiter each day, how much time is spent with each candidate, and more and more. When I was at Deloitte, management wanted to track how much time each recruiter spent in the ATS-aughh!

Most hiring managers like the idea of a recruiting scorecard with key metrics. Recruiters are often less enthusiastic, and I can understand why. The traditional metrics can be kept in such a way that it's tough to show you're doing a good job.

That isn't the intention, of course, but as all of our discussions have revealed, there can be unintended interpretations of what's said or what the data is really showing.

So regardless of where you and your organization fall on the continuum of metrics keeping, let's talk about a few metrics that really matter. These metrics will in fact do more than just report what is happening. They will also show the hiring manager the role they play and the impact they have on recruiting success. They also give the hiring manager a good sense of your role and your contribution to their success. And you won't have to say a word!

**Time to *find* vs time to *fill***

The first metric I suggest is a variation on the old stand-by "time to fill." I have an issue with just recording the date the requisition is opened and the date it's closed. The issue? Rarely is the recruiter really the only person responsible for that timeline, whether it's fast or slow.

> *Hiring managers are eager to fill their openings quickly to ensure their businesses can deliver results…but they often don't understand all the legwork required to fill a position.*
>
> *Recruiters, on the other hand, are often measured on key metrics such as time to fill …but they have no control over how fast a hiring manager responds to their requests to review resumes, set up interviews, made an offer, etc.*

There are a lot of factors that influence how quickly a position is filled. To name a few (and I'm sure you can), we could be talking about:

- Poorly written job description so candidates presented were not acceptable to the hiring manager or great candidates were not interested in the job.
- Hiring manager delayed making decisions.
- Candidates were lost for a variety of reasons, but lost is lost.
- Recruiter had too many requisitions to do much sourcing for any of them and had to rely on postings.
- Position was put on hold and/or requirements were changed.

So keeping some kind of notes on the progress of a search is a good thing when you suspect it's going to show up on your performance review and/or recruiting scorecard.

I suggest breaking this metric into sections to help understand where delays are negatively impacting the statistics by which recruiters are being evaluated. This allows you to see where the process got delayed.

Usually by the time you have filled the position, these delays along the way have been forgotten. Now you have a long "time to fill" statistic and no way to explain it nor change it for the next requisition.

The reasons why the timeline is long may vary with hiring managers. Some may take a long time from when the requisition was approved to get you the information you need to start the search. Some may need to see more candidates even though they think they have found the winning candidate—and eventually make an offer to that person. Perhaps there are significant changes in the requirements in the middle of the search.

If a requisition is opened and you wait two weeks for the job description and/or meeting with the hiring manager to get information you need to really start the search, then in reality the search started at that point, not two weeks ago. Just note the date you had the information you needed and were able to start the search.

This is not to lay blame on the hiring manager but to help you, and perhaps your manager, see what's really happening in the search process. And it helps you identify areas where you can shorten the time line by using these techniques to influence the hiring manager. You can improve any of the statistics that don't meet the threshold your company has set.

**Metrics to Show What it Really Takes to Do the Search (See Recruiting Funnel Form)**

Every time I've seen this form presented, it elicits gasps from hiring managers. It tells a big story in a gentle, easy to understand way. And it shows the role of the hiring manager in the overall search timeline. What's not to like?

If you have a system that is keeping track of these numbers for you, then you may be able to show this to your hiring manager at the beginning of a search. If not, showing the hiring manager this information during the search will be useful. Showing it to them at the end of the search can be mind blowing—to everyone involved!

This form will help you and the hiring manager pinpoint where any issues with each search may lie. These numbers point out areas of potential improvement that will ultimately improve the entire process.

*We were engaged to help a small technology company improve their recruiting process. One of their biggest complaints was, you can probably guess, time to fill a position. Their diagnosis was that the recruiter was not bringing candidates fast enough.*

*So the CEO wanted me to do some "recruiting" coaching for the recruiter. But of course, you and I can guess that the first place to look is hiring manager behavior.*

*So we gathered the data for this form for one recent requisition that had seemingly taken nearly six months to fill. And right there, on one page, the data pointed out the main problem area. The company was extending 4-5 offers to get one hire. No wonder it took forever to fill a position. (We used the Recruiting Funnel diagram I've given you at the back.)*

*Here is what is startling! The recruiter had actually done the job 4 times! It was something else that had kept the position open for so long.*

*When we examined what was happening, we learned the hiring manager was making very low offers. The lower the salaries he was paying, the better his profitability-a key KPI in his performance evaluation.*

*At the same time, he had several open positions which were impacting profitability. The recruiter had not been able to have a conversation with him about the impact the low offers were having on the speed of filling the position. He simply didn't believe her.*

*But now we could have a simple conversation with numbers that showed what was happening. Turns out he actually thought 4-5 offers for one acceptance was an industry standard! Yikes, how would they keep a company going with statistics like that?*

*Also, it was clear to everyone that this was not a recruiter issue, unlike their initial assessment.*

*This happens in some companies. Hiring managers can be between a rock and a hard place when they are evaluated something actually counter to fast hiring.*

## Timeline Expectations

During the initial discussion you have with the hiring manager, ask about their expectations of how long it will take to get to major milestones in the search. It's a great strategy to get those expectations out into the open. Often manager won't tell you unless you ask. But they won't be happy if you don't meet them.

Finally, remember the "start with the end in mind" strategy. What metrics are important to the hiring manager? Ask them.

They quite likely have some desired timeframes and numbers of candidates they would like to see. They may not share those expectations and preferences with you unless you ask. It's going to be hard to meet if you don't know what they are!

You can agree, modify, or "see what the market tells us" when you know the metrics that matter to your hiring manager.

John is a fabulous recruiter and friend. His approach is to set various timelines during the initial conversation, and then he keeps discussing them with the hiring manager and updating them as necessary throughout the entire search process. That really helps develop a business partner relationship and accountability for the process at the same time!

Another way to use the funnel is to lay out the expected timeline. As you fill in the numbers on the right, this is a great way for you and the hiring manager to clearly see what's happening with the search, where the issues are, where requirements and/or timelines may need to be changed, and more.

Hiring managers are busy, and to get their attention in a meaningful way, a diagram may be just what you need.

In the next technique, I want to share a tip I learned from a housecleaning chemical salesman on building trust. It's incredibly simple, rarely done, and powerful. Try it just once and you'll see how helpful it is.

# Technique 12: Fastest Way to Build Trust and Credibility

Building trust and credibility quickly can be a challenge. As we've already discussed, people often think the only way to do that is to bring in the right number of the right candidates. Obviously that is important, yet it also takes some time. What if there were easy ways to more quickly start building trust and credibility with your hiring managers? Here are a few examples that I hope you will try. Feel free to modify them to fit your situation. They really do work.

First, let me start with the secret of how a salesman became a millionaire with one simple technique. What he shared with me can be very effective in creating successful partnership relationships.

*Sometime ago I met Marty, a salesman who had become a millionaire selling chemicals to companies who cleaned offices. I had certainly never thought selling office-cleaning chemicals was a millionaire-making profession. I just had to know what the secret to his success was. He revealed to me that it was because everyone trusted him.*

*So, as I'm sure you can predict, I asked him how that trust had been created. And he shared an astonishingly simple technique. He simply did what he promised he would do when he promised he would do it.*

*He did it pretty elaborately, but as you get the gist of how he created trust, it will be relatively easy to implement. He would set up a meeting with a prospective client for a few days away. Then he would call the day before to remind them he would be at their office at a certain time and day. Just before he was to meet with them, he would call again saying he would be there at the time they had agreed upon. When he met the prospect, he would say, "Here I am as I promised."*

Now that may seem like overkill, but it left the clear impression with the prospective client that this salesperson did what he said he would do and when he said he would do it. Think about how rare that is in the world today. So if you have a hiring manager with whom you want to quickly build trust, this is one step that will make a difference.

Make a promise to do something you know you can do at the specified time. Then deliver. And point out that as promised, you did what you said you would. You won't have to do it so often it gets obnoxious. Just once or twice and you will have created your reputation as someone who does what they promise.

**How under-promising and over-delivering can get you in trouble over time**

This is discussed in more detail in the Recruiting Good Intentions section earlier. Just a quick reminder:

I know lots of people say it's a way to success, but I have also seen it wipe out credibility. How does that happen?

The first time you under promise and over deliver, people may be really happy about it. By the second time you do it, you are starting to create an expectation that you will always perform this way.

So while that may make people happy in the short run, it confuses them in the long run. Can you be trusted to tell them the truth or are you always holding back a little? When you say it will take a week to accomplish something, is that how long it really takes? Or are you just adding some extra time so you look good when you get it done in three days?

Quality can be defined as doing what you say you will do, when you say you will do it. It doesn't require over-delivering. That's great to do from time to time. It just isn't something you want to train people to expect on a regular basis.

In Marty's story above, you will see he promised exactly what he delivered exactly when he delivers. That consistency will make all the difference.

**Let me take a little more time so this gets the attention it deserves.**

Sometimes you may also not want to be the fastest one to deliver. Here's another story.

> *I worked with a tax accountant many years ago who had built a very large tax practice of nearly 1000 client with two simple marketing concepts. The first was amazingly subtle and effective—and free.*
>
> *I would do the returns first and estimate the tax due or the refund. Then the taxpayers would be escorted to the tax accountant's office for a quick review of their return. He saw every one of his clients, though often for no more than 2-3 minutes.*
>
> *He would tell them, "We could go with this return now, but I'd like to take another day or so to review it personally. That way we will make sure we've done the very best job possible for you." He did spend a few minutes reviewing their information. But it was clearly the fact that he would take the time he needed to do a good job that impressed his clients.*
>
> *And the clients loved it. Even though there would be a delay in the processing, they felt he was giving them some personal and extra attention. They would tell me over and over how special he made them feel.*

It clearly showed that sometimes it makes sense to NOT respond quickly.

I tell you this in case there are times you want to take a little more time to give something the extra attention it deserves. We use this approach when it comes to writing the posting for a search using the information we learned in the launch meeting.

Often the hiring manager wants to see the document in a day or so. We probably could get it done in that timeframe, but it wouldn't be the quality document we want. So we say something like "I would like to take an extra day to give this the attention it deserves. It's an important document and I want to do the very best job possible."

When you do that, it's essential that you stick to your timeframe. The discussion on under-promising and over-delivering explained why keeping to an agreed-upon timeframe is essential to the building of your relationship of credibility and trust.

> *What was the other marketing technique this incredible tax accountant used to build his business? Personally, I never quite understood the magic of this, but people loved it nearly as much as they did the first technique.*
>
> *Every year he and his wife traveled to several exotic locations during the summer. And every year each client got a postcard from that year's location.*
>
> *As I said, people loved it. I would hear client after client say, "I got your postcard. Thank you."*

Regarding that second strategy--I'd love to think the message here is for you to take a glorious vacation and send your hiring managers postcards, but …

In the next technique, let's talk about the "push back."

As recruiters, we often get lots of advice to push back on your hiring managers in certain situations. However, you undoubtedly realize that when you push someone, in any way, they often push back! I want to show you a "non-push back" gets you what you really wanted all along!

# Technique 13: The Art of the Push-Back-- Without Pushing Back.

Hiring managers want something that we know doesn't exist, won't work, or is just a bad idea. For example they might ask for:

- A highly skilled candidate but only want to pay a salary more in line for someone less skilled
- A combination of skills where the demand is much higher than the supply
- A career history that is rare if it even exits—ever have a hiring manager who said they wouldn't consider anyone who had spent less than five years in each position or someone who only had two positions in their entire career?
- A skill set that is clearly not what is required for the position—our hiring manager, the finance VP of a large distribution company, liked the idea of having a CPA in the finance director role, not because it was necessary but because there were no other CPAs in the company. Of course, many people in finance do not have a CPA.
- A skill set that requires more years of experience than the years the hiring manager is asking for—our client, a worldwide entertainment company, asked for human resources manager candidates with experience that typically only people at the director level and above would have.
- An interview process that seems to include everyone but the night crew.
- An interview process that does not acknowledge the realities of the market demand for certain types of experience—our client wanted to hold all candidates until they had a "slate," even if they lost candidates during that protracted interview process.

You can probably add a lot of items to this list.

Effective, non-confrontational "push back" starts as soon as you hear something that seems a little--or a lot--outrageous. You don't have to argue about whether the hiring manager's expectations are reasonable at this point. You can (and should) plant some little seeds that will grow.

Here's an example you can probably relate to. We have a client who felt candidates should be so delighted and grateful to be working for them that they would take positions for less than they were making. So when we launched the search, we didn't say "You must be kidding." We wanted to but…

First, ask questions to explore how they have arrived at whatever they think they want to offer. So we asked the hiring manager questions like:

- Is it your experience that people TODAY can afford to take a step back in compensation?
- Have you seen candidates who had EVERYTHING you're asking for in that salary range or have you hired candidates who met all your requirements in that range?
- If someone is right on target in terms of their experience and skills, is there any flexibility in that range?

When you just ask for more information and truly want to know how the hiring manager came to certain conclusions, you'll often learn the real story, which will make life much easier for you. What we learned is that the hiring manager was worried about salary compression. He reluctantly admitted that he realized qualified candidates would probably be more expensive, but was hoping the search would turn up some great candidates at his deflated price.

Once you know these critical pieces of information, you and your hiring manager are on the same side. Now you can talk to them about their concerns, and your chances of being successful have just increased dramatically. Of course, there are hiring managers who are out of touch with the world today. Whichever kind you have, here's the next step.

What you do now is say something like: "I can understand your issues (or preferences) on compensation. How about this? We'll go to the market and see what viable candidates are making today. We'll bring you everyone who is qualified and in your salary range, if they are out there. We'll show you candidates in your salary range who are as close to the qualifications as possible. We'll also bring you information about what qualified candidates are making. Then you can see what those extra dollars will buy you. Would that be helpful?"

This always elicits a sigh of relief from the hiring manager. They are so used to recruiters just saying either OK and trying for months to find that dream candidate or saying NO without coming up with a viable alternative strategy. Here's where you really demonstrate your skill as the recruiting consultant and their business partner.

No matter what your hiring manager has been unrealistic or unreasonable about, you can plant these seeds. The seeds that say, "I'm concerned about this for the following reason. Here is how we can see if this is in the marketplace. Let's look at the people who show interest in this position, and then we can decide."

**What if you didn't realize something would be an issue?**

At the back I've given you a form you can follow to deliver "bad" news. This form is especially useful when you and the hiring manager have to come to agreement on what needs to happen, and for those times when you need to be able to have a frank discussion about changes the hiring manager may need to make. This form will help you slide right into that conversation, get the hiring manager to participate in crafting a solution, and even strengthen your relationship.

Now we need to talk about the overworked and often ignored concept of the candidate experience. Most hiring managers consider this your responsibility, by the way. Here's how to share the duties.

# Technique 14: How to Get Everyone to Support You to Create a Great Candidate Experience

The candidate experience for all applicants, regardless of whether they are the winning candidate, at all touch points in the process, should be a reflection of your employment brand. The candidate experience is a major portion of the evidence the candidate gathers about what it would be like to work for your company.

In today's wild economy, I see some companies and hiring managers seeming to adopt an attitude of "there are so many candidates I don't need to worry about how they are treated." That attitude can have wide and long lasting impact in the candidate community to say nothing about the issues it creates for you as the recruiter. Perhaps even with that attitude your hiring manager will be able to get people to take the job, but you and I both know what's going to happen in the future..

At the same time, there is real pressure on certain positions because the demand is far greater than the number of people who can meet it. You probably have some positions that fall into this category. I've been coaching recruiters at some of the most admired, prestigious and household name companies. What is a huge problem they are facing?

They have traditionally relied on the well-known brand name of their company as a way to attract candidates. Now, with such pressure in certain areas, that brand name is not working. For some positions, it is actually working against them because candidates think they know the company and don't see it as a place to advance their career.

Some of the hiring managers are still thinking that because it's such a famous company, candidates are just lining up and will put up with whatever they have to in order to work at the company. You can probably relate to how crazy that makes the recruiters!

So improving the candidate experience is important, speeding up all aspects of the process, streamlining the interview schedules, etc. And the recruiters are determined to get all of those things to happen.

My advice to them: Use all these tools and at the same time **never use the term** *candidate experience*.

That term is one you will probably never hear a hiring manager use, and their eyes may just glaze over if you use it. They just don't like the term—and may not like the concept much. It's a little like fingernails on a blackboard to many people.

They don't intentionally mistreat candidates; they just don't relate to it nor see it as inappropriate.

So can recruiters influence the candidate experience? I think we absolutely can. As you ask questions, guide the hiring managers, build strong partnerships, you will have the ultimate influence on improving the candidate experience.

Just do it without using the term "candidate experience." ☺

Here is some information that will give you additional ways to think about this, and maybe tidbits and sound bites to sprinkle into your conversation.

A nationwide research project determined that the quality of the candidate experience is the key decision factor in whether a candidate accepts an offer. The formula:

(Job content + compensation + work/life balance) multiplied by the candidate experience = candidate's feelings about working for your company

A recent quote from a nationally known author on recruiting: "*Applicants are not stupid. They realize that 90% of companies treat applicants worse than most people treat their pet dog. Because applicants know the rules and where the power resides, they generally accept the indifferent treatment [they] receive during the recruiting process.*"

Most "A" players believe that it is obvious they are the best. While the hiring manager and interview team certainly must engage in an interview and assessment process, it is important to recognize that strong players want to be "courted."

It is crucial to have a recruiting process that is perceived as sensitive to the candidate and "high touch". A process with those qualities will successfully project the company's brand and help insure that at the end of the process, the candidate will still be excited about working for your company.

# WHY FINDING GREAT CANDIDATES IS NOT ENOUGH

## Use This Woefully Neglected Factor to Skyrocket Your Recruiting Results

## KATHERINE MOODY

Author: The Consultative Recruiter
Creator: Epic Results Recruiting Master Class

# Bonus Report 1: Why Finding Great Candidates Isn't Enough

**Off with Their Heads**

When in doubt
it's off with their heads


It's the least I can do
off with their heads
Is the only phrase that always rings true
Never gets old
So I say to you
With conviction
Off with their heads.

*Queen of Hearts from Disney's "Alice in Wonderland"*

# Introduction

For several years, I've worked with many companies to share my unique recruiting techniques and strategies to improve time to fill, bring more great candidates to the table, and equally important smooth and strengthen the relationship between recruiters and their hiring managers.

It's scary how often I hear hiring managers say they feel the only solution to the problems with recruiting would be to fire all the recruiters and just start all over again. In fact, I recently did a Consultative Recruiting workshop for a recruiting team where the Talent Acquisition Director had done just that—had totally turned over her team of 10 in the last few months.

And that hadn't changed a thing!

If you were to do a survey of your hiring managers, while they might stop short of "off with their heads," they probably do have significant concerns and frustration. At the same time, I know most recruiters have significant concerns and frustrations as well. I'll bet there are times you've had the same dreams of "off with their heads" though you are thinking of a different group!

## Surprising #1 Predictor of Talent Acquisition Performance

Bersin Research at Deloitte conducted extensive research to determine what factors impacted talent acquisition performance and results.

In a comparison of 15 recruiting tools and strategies, it was clear that the strategy that had the most influence on recruiting success was the relationship between the recruiter and hiring managers. They found that it was actually FOUR TIMES more important than the other 14 factors combined!

Through their interviews, they found that the majority of TA leaders agree that recruiters who have the closest relationships with hiring managers outperform recruiters who do not have such close relationships.

There is a lot of focus on the candidate-side of the recruiting function. This research was considered "surprising", but I bet most recruiters are not at all surprised with these findings.

It is my experience that:

a) TA leaders are often unable to show recruiters how to build those relationships and instead give advice like "push back on the hiring manager," "take more control," or "tell the hiring manager about our SLA or other process", and

b) recruiters think that working hard and filling reqs will eventually build those essential relationships.

By now we have to admit neither of these are effective strategies to build relationships of credibility and influence with your hiring managers.

Despite evidence that these relationships are in disarray as evidenced by things like unacceptably long times to fill, hiring managers who do not respond to recruiter requests and a myriad of struggles to fill positions, a 2014 study by ERE Media found that while recruiters and hiring managers have different views of recruiter performance—*with recruiters giving themselves an average performance grade of B and hiring managers giving recruiters an average grade of C-plus.*

## The Cycle that Negatively Impacts Recruiting Success

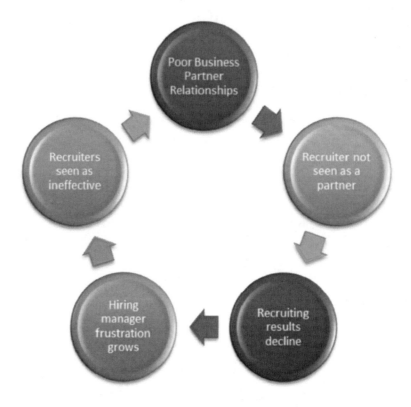

# Business Only Gets Done Through Relationships

Successful people believe their success is attributable to a pattern of mutually beneficial interpersonal relationships, perhaps even more than their technical skills or business knowledge. These relationships are not the ones dictated by the organizational chart, by the way.

*"Improving…relationships is important for sustained high performance."* Susan Fowler, a senior consulting partner with The Ken Blanchard Companies

Your success will always be based on the degree to which you are trusted by your stakeholders.

*The Trusted Advisor*
*Charles Green &*
*Andrea Howe*

Recruiters and hiring managers often have weak, even dysfunctional, business partner relationships. So while poor relationships create recruiting problems, great relationships can be the solutions to those problems.

**NEW! Video Master Class  Epic Result Recruiting: Exactly What You Can Do to Eliminate Forever the Undeserved Stereotype of "Order Taker" and Start Having More Influence and Credibility with Your Hiring Managers**

**Check it out!**

https://the-consultative-recruiter.teachable.com/p/how-to-leverage-ai-tools-to-become-a-consultative-recruiter

## Signs Your Recruiting Will Benefit from Better Relationships

Perhaps you've heard some of these almost universal complaints about recruiting in your organization or have experienced these yourself:

- Time to fill is too long—according to your time to fill requirements and/or hiring managers!
- Hiring managers do not feel they see enough qualified candidates and ask for  more, more more!
- Recruiters are spending a lot of time trying to hunt down hiring managers who do not get back to them
- Hiring managers do not give enough feedback on the candidates they interview or resumes they receive
- Recruiters do not have sufficient time with a hiring manager to discuss a new requisition so inappropriate candidates get presented; the search may stop and start over a long time, etc.
- Recruiters are frustrated because hiring managers do not follow the agreed-upon "process"
- Hiring managers would not give their recruiters high marks on a recruiting satisfaction survey

If any of this sounds familiar, it's no wonder you may feel frustrated and unappreciated because hiring managers do not seem to value your expertise. There can be many different reasons for these complaints, but for sure your hiring manager relationships are a major factor.

So here is an unfortunate but common example of what does happen in the real world:

## A Recruiter Success Evaluated by Her Boss as a Recruiter Failure

*While doing searches for a worldwide technology company where the "off with their heads" hiring manager sentiment was really beginning to build, I was talking to a recruiter who was feeling very discouraged and frustrated.*

*Despite having been a recruiter for several years and doing what she thought was good work, she had just been told that her upcoming performance review was going to be quite negative. Her hiring managers were very unhappy with her and were complaining loudly and frequently to the VP HR who managed the recruiting function.*

*So the recruiter and I analyzed one of the searches she had been doing for one of her most critical hiring managers. There was no denying the time to fill was embarrassing long, especially painful and visible since this was such a mission-critical position for that hiring manager who was implementing a major new strategy for the organization.*

*As we talked about the search, two things became clear.*

1. *She was actually terrified of the hiring manager, and never talked to him unless things were blowing up. She didn't have a business partnership with him, didn't think he respected her and would never think of doing anything even close to a "push back."*
2. *There had been four people the hiring manager liked enough to make an offer. In a sense, she had actually filled the job three times! All while having the reputation of not being able to get the job done!*

*All the offers had been turned down, for various reasons. So while the recruiter had important information that should have been shared with the hiring manager throughout the entire process, she had never been able to have those critical conversations.*

*Their relationship had deteriorated to the point where she avoided him, and he discounted her perspective and advice. Of course that really means he had lost trust and confidence in her as a recruiter. And he made his unhappiness very visible—loudly--to the VP HR.*

*Naturally, the VP HR didn't like getting complaints about the recruiter and did not enjoy being yelled at by the hiring manager even more! It was easy to come to the conclusion the recruiter was simply not doing a good job.*

*The VP continually coached the recruiter to "push back" with the hiring manager in a desperate attempt to salvage the relationship and of course to stop the complaints she was getting. As you can imagine, the recruiter was convinced there was no way she was going to try that!*

*Eventually, the only solution the VP came up with was to give the recruiter a negative review—which wasn't an accurate reflection of her ability to bring in candidates.*

## The Elephant Still in the Room

*Broken relationships are at the root of many of the perceived issues with recruiting and create many of the challenges recruiters face every day.*

As recruiters, we were taught and/or came to believe that finding good candidates is the key to closing reqs fast which will lead to business partnership relationships with happy hiring managers . Every recruiter I've known works hard to bring in great candidates.

Then they (and me at one time) believe/hope that if we can just do that enough times, we will be seen as trusted advisors. Let the good relationships will begin!

Of course there is a basic flaw in that reasoning, despite how logical as it appears on the surface.

*Hard work to find and bring great candidates to your company is not sufficient to improve a troubled relationship with your hiring managers.*

It's my experience that people typically talk about recruiting problems in terms of candidate sourcing, time to fill, candidate experience etc., But if we were to talk about the cause of those issues, it becomes clear that the root cause—and thus the solution—is the relationship itself.

It's not easy to know how to address this elephant in the room, even though I suspect everyone knows at some level that it's there. It's easier to retreat to thinking more and/or better candidates will magically make things better. Or maybe we need another recruiter, a new sourcing function or more social media or another Boolean search string for LinkedIn Recruiter.

In other words, your ability to find candidates was the reason you got the job.

And the main reason recruiters have unnecessary time wasters, frustrations and even sometimes reputations as order takers?

Because they were not able to build business partnerships of credibility with their hiring managers, and were not perceived as being able to function as *Consultative Recruiters.*

Here is a critical truth:  It's ironic that this most critical skill--building strong relationships within an organization--is rarely, if ever, taught. Most Talent Acquisition management cannot tell you *how* to be consultative. They just know they want you to be. And your hiring managers want you to be. But they cannot give you concrete directions on exactly how to do that.

It would be easy to be very discouraged or frustrated when you read this. But I wrote this to give you clarity around the real issues, as well as some of the key concepts that will support you as you set forth to build your reputation or the reputation of your team as a Trusted Advisors who operate as the consultants your hiring managers really want.

**I wouldn't promise that building your reputation as a Consultative Recruiter will solve all your recruiting issues. But you will be amazed at how much it does improve your recruiting results. You will see significant and unexpected productivity improvements and multiple benefits in all aspects of your recruiting.**

# The Strategy that Improves Recruiting Results and Satisfaction for All

- Recruiters who have good business partnerships with hiring managers are viewed as trusted, strategic advisors, in other words, consultative recruiters.
- Recruiters who are viewed this way are able to achieve better recruiting results. It actually improves every aspect of the recruiting cycle!

## *Typical But Ultimately Insufficient Strategies*

More Sourcing Avenues?
Often we see companies add more candidate sourcing avenues, such as creating or adding to a sourcing team, adding additional job boards especially those who can deliver jobs to candidate mobile devices, LinkedIn Recruiter, various services that tweet your jobs to candidates, Facebook company pages, etc., as ways to meet the hiring managers' needs.

Of course it's important for recruiters to understand how to leverage all the new ways to generate candidates. But if your relationships with hiring managers are not working, I know you realize the solution isn't yet another cool way to find great candidates. The solution also is not about finding more and more candidates for a position. If finding and assessing great candidates were sufficient, these frustrations and problems would have been eliminated long ago.

Creating a "Process" or Implementing an SLA?
Sometimes there is a lot of effort put into defining and building a big recruiting process map. Then the hiring managers are "invited" to a meeting to learn the recruiting process. There often is an incredible investment of time in

this, and honest and good commitments from all involved. But often the expectations set out and the commitments made in those meetings are rarely met.

You may have had a similar experience. So if a meeting to discuss recruiting process were sufficient to improve recruiting, it would have happened by now.

**Score Card?**

Some companies implement a score card process. There can be great value for recruiters and hiring managers in a score card process; however, we've found two issues with the traditional approaches to measuring recruiting results.

- The wrong things are measured and critical things are not reflected, so time to fill statistics are totally inaccurate.
- There is really no significant improvement in the relationships between recruiting and hiring managers so no change in the issues.

These things may get marginal results. But don't settle for "marginal". There is an easy and fast way to equip yourself with the tools and techniques that will get your hiring managers to see you as their Trusted Advisor, and you see dramatically increased recruiting results.

## *An Example of Consultative Recruiting*

### When sourcing seems to be the problem but isn't the solution

Countless times recruiters tell me they need better and/or more ways to source candidates. This understandably seems to be the solution when:

- Searches have been open for a long time, and everyone is unhappy with how things are going
- The hiring manager rejects candidates the recruiter thinks fit the requirements
- Changes are made to title, requirements, and/or duties in an attempt to attract qualified candidates without any input from the recruiter
- The recruiter is sending many LinkedIn Inmails with very low response
- If you could say it without looking bad, you would admit you aren't really sure what the position does and/ or what the hiring manager is looking for. Knowing what you don't know is a great place to start getting this search back on track.

So it's very natural for everyone to think it's a matter of putting more emphasis on sourcing--*everyone* being the hiring manager, the recruiter and the recruiter's manager. So the pressure is on for you to do more of what isn't working.

And of course in one way it would be great if "sourcing" was the answer, because the answer I'm suggesting can feel harder to do than hiding out in "more sourcing activities, new job boards, etc." {I know. I've done that myself.}

To start at the right place to get the search back on track:

1. Have the launch meeting/call with the hiring manager. Call it a mid-course calibration or the "I have a few questions so we can more closely target candidates" conversation. No need to throw anyone under the bus here, including you. (For a list of some excellent questions, please see the Question Library in this book. It has all the questions you'll ever need!)

2. Make sure you ask the questions you have without apology or feeling stupid for having them. NOTE: I've been recruiting for more years than I want to see in writing and absolutely have never seen a job description that gave me the information I needed to do a quality search.

3. Rewrite the posting as if you were talking to the ideal candidate and explaining the position and what makes it a great opportunity for them.

4. Rewrite your Inmail message with a subject line that your ideal candidates cannot resist and a link to the new engaging posting .

Only after these steps, can you determine what sourcing changes you need, if any.

Here is another great story of how one recruiter got a search on track . She used the steps above and she and her hiring manager were delighted with the results!

Recruiter as Trusted Advisor: Case Study

PH., talent acquisition recruiter, Consumer Technology

Search status:

- The req had been open for 2 months, with no hires.
- Recruiter was new to the location, the candidate pool in that area, and this was her first search for the hiring manager.
- Even though recruiter was not getting results, she afraid to do anything that might rock the boat, so her only strategy was to post and pray.
- The recruiter phone screened 12, the hiring manager reluctantly interviewed 3 of those, but none were a fit for the position.

Actions taken:

- Took matters into her own hands and requested an hour meeting with the HRBP and the hiring manager
- Used the launch document questions to do a deep dive into the position, learn what they really wanted, etc.
- Rewrote the posting to be candidate- and marketing-focused, got approval of the new posting from the hiring manager and reposted.

Results:

- Position was filled in 3 weeks
- Double the number of qualified candidates applied to the new posting.
- What she told me: "Before I decided to use the tools Katherine gave me, I had reviewed 150 resumes with no hires. Now 3 weeks later, the position is filled and the hiring manager is very happy!"

Impact on hiring manager-recruiter relationship:
*"Instead of an having an unhappy hiring manager, this simple change has improved my relationship in a matter of weeks. Plus we filled the position quickly!"*

**Recap:**

- 2 months after the req was opened, the recruiter had reviewed over 150 resumes; only 12 strong enough to be screened by recruiter and 3 were moved forward to be interviewed by hiring manager.
- The hiring manager interviewed and rejected those 3 candidates
- People were no longer applying to the posting.
- Within 3 weeks of using The Consultative Recruiter tools and techniques, the position was filled.

NOTE: She has decided not to do any more of the "post and pray" recruiting but to continue to used the tools and techniques. They saved her time, filled the position more quickly than it would have been using the old style recruiting and created a happy hiring manager.

---

**More Qualified Candidates—Better Hiring Manager Relationships—Faster Times to Fill**

*The Consultative Recruiter: The Recruiting Strategies that Change Everything*

**Call or email to discuss training and coaching:**

Katherine@ConsultativeRecruiting.com

**832.464.4447**

---

# HOW
# TO
# HAVE
# YOUR
# BEST
# SEARCH
# EVER!

THE CONSULTATIVE RECRUITER

# Bonus Report 2: How to Have Your Best Search Ever

*Infographic: Recruiting Fail Points*

Here is what one recruiter told me after her first launch meeting:

*"I have to tell you- that was the best launch meeting I have ever had. The hiring manager said she was thoroughly impressed with the process, the level of detail I was digging into, and that this was the most in-depth discussion she had had to date about a position when hiring for it. From this particular manager, especially, this was a huge compliment."*

*HB, Talent Acquisition Consultant*

## How a Good Launch Results in a Great Hire—and Faster Time to Fill

The launch meeting is where and how you get the information you need for:

→ Creating engaging postings as well as descriptions for your company's career page that separate your positions from the "pack"
→ Generating a higher level of interest from more of the right candidates
→ Screenings that designed to get you more information in less time
→ Resolving "I'll know it when I see it." & "Send more resumes."

Plus, it is THE perfect time to start your "commitment" strategy to avoid wasting time tracking down feedback about candidates from your hiring managers.

NOTE: Please check out Strategy Technique #1 at the end of this document. You'll be amazed at how easy and effective this approach can be.

In the launch meeting, you will be able to get hiring managers talking about what's new that they are excited about, what challenges they see, etc. Clearly this information will help you create postings and career page position descriptions that will be exciting to your target candidates. These conversations will often lead to first-time ever real conversations with your hiring managers that go beyond the immediate search. Relationship-building at its best.

Subtly build the image you want them to have of you and the relationship you are creating with them. Remember I said earlier that consultants ask questions not only to get information but to build their image as strong, smart consultants. These questions will help you do exactly that. You know you're building that same reputation when you hear your hiring managers say things like:

• That's a good question.
• I didn't think about that before.
• I need to think about that for a minute.
• No one has asked me that question before.

### *Ask Even if You Know*

#### *#1: What Makes It Great?*

This question is essential for you to ask, for many reasons.
**Often the hiring manager will respond with pretty standard and trite phrases.**
These will not help convince the candidate this is their best career move if the hiring manager isn't able to talk about the role, the team, the company, the future, etc.

If you work for a company everyone knows, that can be helpful, but it can also be a challenge. Why? Because your hiring managers think "everyone wants to work here" and may not understand that for certain positions, that isn't true. So you can help "train" your hiring managers but first you have to know what they are saying.

*I worked with a company recently that claimed to be the nation's largest distributor of their products. Ironically that wasn't the case at all; that statement was something the marketing department had decided to put on their website. Even stranger was that the hiring managers acted as if it were true. They felt that statement was all the evidence a candidate would need to decide to become an employee! Needless to say, they needed some "training" around what additional information to add to their discussion with candidates.*

For those of you with inquiring minds, NO, I was not able to get them to take that statement off their website! But we surely changed the conversation with the candidates. Interestingly, what you will experience by having these conversations is that, even if they don't make the change you suggested, they will be more receptive to your next suggestion. So even if you lose this one, rest assured you're going to win more in the future.

**This is a time where you can have critical conversations with your hiring manager that will impact and improve your search and your image as a consultative recruiter.**
Now is when you share what you know their ideal candidates will be looking for, what the position has to have in order to be exciting to the target candidates, etc. You can point out what the position (team, company, future, etc.) has that the ideal candidates are longing to find.

As you share what you know will be necessary to attract the best candidates, you are certainly training your hiring managers. Interestingly, you are demonstrating your expertise and knowledge of the candidate pool at the same time.

**It's a great way to continue to build your image of the consultative recruiter.**

The launch document I've shared with you at the end of this report and in the documents report is a library of questions I've compiled and tested in my nearly 25+ years of recruiting. They are going get you great information, perhaps some you've never heard before. And they strengthen your image as the hiring manager's consultative recruiter.

*#2: What is the reason your ideal candidate will be interested?*

This may seem like the same question, but it is slightly different and you ask it to start a different conversation. This is the best way to talk about any unrealistic expectations your hiring manager may have.

## Dealing with Unrealistic Expectations

*The $ needed to get their ideal candidate.*

Often hiring managers, HRPBs and even corporate compensation committees have no concept of what a competitive compensation range needs to be. For example, some companies pride themselves on paying, say, 75%-80% of the market target salary for positions. For those positions where the candidate pool is small and/or in high demand, this standard may result in a longer search.

This is a place where you can truly serve as a consultant to your hiring manager.
The magic question that I found hiring managers related to was something like the following points:

1. As you probably know, when people are used to making a certain salary, they have most likely created a lifestyle that meets that salary.

2.  Most people need their current salary to support their expenses and obligations.

3.  Do you find that it's easy for people to live for some unspecified period of time on only a percentage of what they need for their current lifestyle?

4.  How would that work?

5.  And are we opening ourselves up to an unhappy employee who may start looking elsewhere when they see their new paycheck amount?

I had several searches for a prestigious company that had exactly that standard. By having this conversation early in the launch process, we got it on the table. Turns out the hiring manager was going crazy under that standard. In "consultant" mode I offered a strategy that could potentially make a change.[1]

Even if you cannot get the compensation changed, you've made the point that there probably won't be a huge stream of candidates raising their hand for this situation.

### What ideal candidates are looking for in this kind of role.

For example, in most technology roles, people like to know they are working with start of the art technology, work on exciting projects, and have smart team mates. If that's not the case for the position you're talking about, you will want to let the hiring manager know what people are looking for, and help come up with a way to give the target candidates something they are looking for. Otherwise they will go somewhere else, as you know. But your hiring manager may not know that or be willing to admit it. So this conversation is critical to have, and have it early in the process—at the launch meeting.

### What candidates are willing to give up to join the company

One company I worked for liked the idea of bringing people on at a lower level than the one they currently had. It was some sort of motivation-promotion-?? strategy they had fallen in love with.

Of course, many of the best candidates were not so in love with the idea. By asking the hiring manager how they would explain to a candidate at, say, a Vice President level, why a Director title was a good career move, the hiring manager began to get a sense of why the best candidates might not be willing to do that to their career. In fact, he said "I'm not sure I would be willing to take that step back just to work here."

---

[1] Because I had this candid conversation about the compensation range and what candidates were actually making, my hiring manager admitted to me that this policy was severely hampering his hiring efforts. We agreed that I would present candidates within the company range, but also present a few candidates who had the skill set but were above the range. Then he (and the compensation department) could see "what the extra dollars would buy them in the marketplace."

He was delighted that there would finally be real life evidence of what the going rate in the marketplace really was for his positions. This approach did help get the compensation range increased, and the hiring manager and I had a great working relationship that started with that conversation during the launch meeting.

I did this with multiple hiring managers within the company, and have used it many times since.

Even when I wasn't working on his searches, he would seek me out to ask my advice on his hiring situations. That's when you know you are seen as a consultative recruiter!

So we still looked for people at the VP level for this Director position, but the hiring manager agreed to look at people who currently had a Director title. That considerably shortened the time it took to find a great candidate who was in a Director level position.

That is not to imply that this conversation will get the change you are looking for. You'll have times where the hiring manager begins to understand the challenges of conducting a search under these conditions, and still won't budge. But you've started the conversation, raised the red flag, and had the important conversation—all of which demonstrates your expertise and the value you bring to the hiring manager.

If there is no way to change things, at least you and the hiring manager have discussed the things that may result in very few candidates expressing interest in the position. This is an important conversation, especially with hiring managers who seem to think "everyone must want to work for us. How hard can it be to recruit for our great company?"

So using questions rather than just trying to *educate* the hiring manager is the best way to:

- Gently show the hiring manager the conflicting elements in what they are looking for
- Share what you know will ideal candidates will say about this.
- Do a little **passive vs active candidates** "training" for your HM
- Get the hiring manager to consider changing requirements, job content, etc. Sometimes adding an additional responsibility, removing a non-essential requirement, or pointing out something great about the opportunity can open up a whole new pool of candidates. I'll bet your hiring manager never would have thought of that without you!

## Solve—or at Least Start the Conversation to Solve--Potential Issues Up Front

In addition to discussing the two items above, this is also the time and ideal format for you to begin to deal with any issues you can predict based on past experience with the hiring manager.

### Hiring Manager Wants More and More People to Interview the Candidate

If you know the hiring manager wants a lot of people to interview the candidate, or learn that during the launch meeting, now is the time to be their consultant. The key is to talk about things that do matter to the hiring manager. But don't guess at what that would be. Use the questions in the Interview section of the launch document, and of course always feel free to modify them in ways that will lead to a conversation about the interview process the hiring manager wants to follow.

I used to talk about "candidate experience" as a way to get hiring managers to create more sensible interview schedules. But now, I wouldn't use that term at all. I know that at some level they do care about that experience. I also know that talking about it as a way to get your hiring managers to change their behavior is really like fingernails on a black board to them.

So this is your opportunity to find their reasons are for those long interview schedules. Once you have that information, it's easier to position your recommendations to help them achieve their goals without subjecting the candidate—and whoever has to schedule all those interviews—to a cumbersome and uncomfortable interview process.

Your goal with this conversation, as with all conversations with your HM, is first to keep building your business relationship and consultative recruiter reputation. The next goal is to have them start to see, with your guidance, the pitfalls and potential issues with their proposed interview process. Then you want to be able to get them to agree to a process that will be the best it can be. That may not mean you get your way and they reduce the number of interviews to what you know makes sense.

Even if you leave with the same number of people involved, if you and the hiring manager have agreed to do things like:

- make sure everyone has seen and agrees with the responsibilities and requirements,
- everyone knows the role they play,
- there is way for the HM to get and evaluate feedback, etc.,

you have provided a HUGE service to the HM.

You don't need to set a goal that you get them to do what you want in just that one meeting. Perhaps you'll get there but if you don't, you have still made great progress. And it's likely that for the next position you work on with that hiring manager, you'll get closer to what you think makes sense.

With this approach you always eventually get to what you want or something even better. Don't set it as a goal, however, because that intention makes it harder for you to have an open, exploring conversation with your hiring manager. Jointly, the two of you may come up with an alternative that is even better than you had originally envisioned. Win-win-win-win….!

Tip: Don't ask who they WANT to be included in the interview schedule. Ask who NEEDS to be included. Just a small language change can start to change your hiring manager's thinking.

### *Just Send Me More…I'll Know It When I See It*

(Be sure to check out the Strategy Techniques later in this book for specific scripts to use for this.)

As you guide the hiring manager to think about and articulate the responsibilities and requirements of the position, you are helping them gain a clarity that will be reflected in a confident hiring decision.

I've found there are several reasons hiring managers may ask for more and more:

- They are afraid to make a bad hiring decision.
- They are losing sight of the requirements for the position.
- They are waiting for a magical "gut feel" about a candidate.

You can probably add more. By the way, I think the statement "This is a bad economy. There should be lots of candidates out there." is actually *code* for one of the reasons above.

The only way you can help your hiring manager overcome their issue is to help them understand the thinking behind it. You do that by (no surprise here) asking questions. You can argue, explain or even just accept their statements, but those choices will never get your hiring manager to make substantive changes. And your time to fill stats won't get better until your hiring managers get past these concerns.

This is truly a situation in which your hiring managers really need you to be their recruiting consultant.

## *How Many Candidates Does the Hiring Manager Need to See*

I will admit that the thought of asking this question can make me—and maybe you as well—nervous. What if they say they want to see tons of candidates? Well, better to know that now than find out later in the search they still want to see more and more.

If you haven't had this upfront conversation, you can explain why there aren't more candidates for the hiring manager to see. The problem is, if you don't explore the number they have mentally decided they want to see up in your launch meeting, when you try to explain why they aren't seeing tons of candidates later in the search, it sounds more like excuses than a discussion about the market realities.

I've seen situations where the position was filled with a great candidate, yet the hiring manager is still unhappy with their recruiter. Why? Because the hiring manager had a mental number of candidates they felt they needed to see, and feel concerned that they didn't get to see enough candidates. The recruiter didn't know that number and had not had the following conversation with the hiring manager. This is one reason that recruiters are filling positions yet their hiring managers are unhappy with them.

Despite what you fear the answer might be, in the launch meeting, ask:

"If the first candidate you meet is a really good fit and meets your qualifications, would you be willing to move forward with an offer?"

If they say no, or say "yes" but don't seem to really mean it, ask: "How many candidates do you feel you would like to see in order to know you've seen the best of those who expressed interest?"

If they have outrageous expectations, this is where you can start to talk about the realities of the market place—competitors, how many candidates will actually meet all the requirements, etc. You can also talk about how the desire to see a significant number of candidates can impact the hiring manager's desired timeframe to fill the position.

Then consider saying something like: Let's go to market with this position and see how many qualified candidates raise their hand and express interest. In a week or so, we'll know what the candidate flow looks like and can see how to move forward so we get a great candidate while adhering as much as possible to your urgency to fill. Would that work for you?

In order to have a move-forward conversation, you need to know what the manager is clear about what they are looking for. As you ask probing questions about the requirements and responsibilities of the position, and talk about the candidate pool, you are helping the hiring manager get clarity around the position.

So later in the search, when (if) your hiring manager is still asking for more and more candidates to interv'
have a comprehensive list of requirements the hiring manager felt were important when you did t¹
down with your hiring manager and that list so the two of you can:

a) Confirm it is still the list. Add, delete and/or clarify based on the resum⸗ has seen.

b) Compare the resumes/candidates you've sent to the hiring manager to aₑ the requirements.

c) Make decisions about the existing resume/candidates

d) Design a move-forward strategy, including coming to an agreement arounα hiring manager will need to see.

124

## Launch Preparation Steps

- Put JD into appropriate sections of Launch Doc
- Identify & highlight statements that seem:
  - → incomplete,
  - → vague,
  - → inappropriate for the position, and/or
  - → out-of-date
- Identify and highlight items to double-check with the hiring manager

## Demystifying the Vague Language of a Job Description

Before showing you a sample of what a launch document looks like after the above preparation, I'd like to talk about the idea of being aware of the issues with the conceptual language used in most job descriptions. Over time, we all seem to have reached an agreement not to ask what that language really means, perhaps thinking we get it because we haven't asked "What does this really mean?".

We think we know what it means, and act as though everyone agrees with our definition. So asking for clarification around the language can be scary or intimidating. What if we're the only one who doesn't get it? Trust me, you won't be the only one. You'll get great information, and your hiring manager will see you in a new way.

### Manages a Team…Everyone Understands That, Right?

I bet I'm not the only one who has seen job descriptions that say something like "manages a team" but nothing about that team. This is one of those say-nothing phrases in job descriptions where you really should ask the hiring manager for the details. It's easy to skip doing that because, after all, we all know what it means to manage a team, right?

Here are the results of asking for details about "manages a team":

- You get a lot of new information for a more interesting posting and on-target screening, and
- You demonstrate your ability to function as a consultative recruiter.

Pick and choose which questions in the team section of the launch document make sense to ask, but don't skip a question because you think it's too basic or because you *think* you know (or should know) the answer. The hiring manager may need to think about some of these questions—that's a sign you've asked a good question.

This is almost a magical list of questions. It shatters any image the hiring manager might have had that you are an order taker. It gets the hiring manager to share information that probably wouldn't have been shared if you hadn't asked these questions.

All of this helps strengthen your business partnership relationship. And that is exactly what you, your management and hiring managers want!

## Preparing a Launch Document Before the Meeting

use this job description for a search done a few years ago for a great VP of Supply Chain at Avery Dennison. complete job description, by the way. Without the information gathered in the launch meeting, I'm pretty ould have been a long and painful search!

## |RECTOR, HUMAN RESOURCES, SUPPLY CHAIN
**Avery Dennison**

**RESPONSIBILITIES:** Responsible for providing overall HR leadership for the Supply Chain organization within Office Products North America division within Avery Dennison. As the primary business partner to the supply chain organization this individual will be responsible driving strategies to maximize the effectiveness of human capital across all manufacturing sites and distribution centers within North America. Serving as a member of the Supply Chain Leadership Team (SCLT) this individual will provide leadership and counsel in the areas of staffing & talent management, training & development, rewards & recognition, performance management, employment law, and employee/labor relations. Lastly, it is expected that this individual drive clear and consistent application of company policies and procedures, and role model Avery Dennison's Code of Business Conduct

- Functional HR leadership of all HR strategies, initiatives, and activities across manufacturing sites, and distribution centers within North America.
- Provide counsel to SCLT on any and all HR-related matters
- Support the VP of Supply Chain, OPNA with strategies, actions and counsel area of organizational development.
- Continually assess supply chain organization and provide recommendations to adjust strategy relating to key human capital levers (e.g. staffing, development, rewards, etc.).
- Serve as a coach to site HR managers in order to ensure they are supported and operating effectively.
- Lead critical cross-site communication and alignment in order to drive strategies, processes and policies consistently and effectively.
- Ensure that managers and employees within the supply chain organization are treated objectively, fairly and with due process
- Personal oversee and/or manage key challenges related to employment law, employee relations and labor relations.
- Strong leadership to help drive and support a continuous improvement culture, consistent with the organization's Enterprise Lean Sigma (ELS) strategy.

### Requirements
- Minimum of eight years experience working in a generalist role, with at least 5 years working in a manufacturing environment. Experience managing multiple locations is strongly preferred
- Experience in operational environment who can relate to factory floor and operational employees Retail/restaurant experience could work.
- Union experience a plus.
- Bachelor's degree in Human Resources or related field. Masters degree preferred.

## Search Launch Form

| POSITION DETAILS | |
|---|---|
| Position Overview | Responsible for providing overall HR leadership for the Supply Chain organization within Office Products North America division within Avery Dennison.<br><br>As the primary business partner to the supply chain organization this individual will be responsible driving strategies to maximize the effectiveness of human capital across all manufacturing sites and distribution centers within North America. How many manuf sites, where located + total ee's<br><br>How many distribution centers, where located + total ee's<br><br>Serving as a member of the Supply Chain Leadership Team (SCLT) who else is on this team? this individual will provide leadership and counsel in the areas of staffing & talent management, training & development, rewards & recognition, performance management, employment law, and employee/labor relations |

Above is a portion of the launch document I created. I copied the position overview into the launch document, and made every sentence a separate paragraph. The reason? Because when there is a lot of data lumped into one big paragraph, I tend to skip over stuff. There is actually research that indicates most people will do the same thing. Do you?

So break things apart so you can really consider them. Think about doing the same thing in your postings, by the way!

Then, as you can see, I've indicated in red my questions and areas where I'm going to ask the hiring manager to tell me more. I want lots of details. Then I can decide how to use that information in postings, screenings, discussions with the hiring manager, etc. The best time and way to get that information is in the launch meeting.

Below you see the responsibilities section with all of my questions, areas where I want additional details, etc. This exploration is critical.

For example, here are some questions you might have around "Coaching to site HR Managers…" etc.

- Are there areas this coaching would need to focus on right away? (lets you know if there are issues in the field HR and hear what the hiring manager thinks of the field HR function)
- Are people likely to be receptive to "coaching"? (good to know what the new director can expect and will be important to add to your screening)
- Is it envisioned that the coaching is done in person or on site when the Director visits?
- Anything that occurs to you as you listen to the hiring manger talk about this point?

Those are the kinds of statements that we think we get what it means, but what does it look like when the new Director is actually doing it? That's so important for you to know what the hiring manager is thinking.

This discussion also helps when you get to requirements. In some job descriptions, the list of requirements is waaay too long. No one is going to read a list of 18 bullets of requirements. In this case, the problem was different. For this relatively high level role, there were exactly 4 requirements listed. You know the hiring manager had a lot more requirements in mind.

By understanding the details of the responsibilities section, you will be able to suggest additional requirements. Then the hiring manager is clear, you know what to look for on a resume and screen for in your interview. This is exactly what will help you find candidates the hiring manager likes and speed up the time to fill!

So based on what I hear from the hiring manager about the Director doing coaching for the Field HR Function, I would talk to the hiring manager about what experience he would like the director to have around coaching. I'm sure he will have an opinion because he will want someone to have some experience coaching a Field HR team. Let's get that defined as a requirement!

| Responsibilities and job duties | |
|---|---|
| | • Functional HR leadership of all HR strategies, initiatives, and activities across manufacturing sites, and distribution centers within North America.<br><br>• Provide counsel to SCLT on any and all HR-related matters Are members of the SCLT used to asking for "counsel"<br><br>• Support the VP of Supply Chain, OPNA with strategies, actions and counsel area of organizational development. What is the nature of "support" required and desired?<br><br>• Continually assess supply chain organization and provide recommendations to adjust strategy relating to key human capital levers (e.g. staffing, development, rewards, etc.)<br><br>• Serve as a coach to site HR managers in order to ensure they are supported and operating effectively.<br><br>• Lead critical cross-site communication and alignment in order to drive strategies, processes and policies consistently and effectively.<br><br>• Ensure that managers and employees within the supply chain organization are treated objectively, fairly and with due process. What is the nature of "ensuring" these things?<br><br>• Personal oversee and/or manage key challenges related to employment law, employee relations and labor relations. Are there any of these "challenges" now? What might these be? |

| Experience and background of the ideal candidate (required, desired, helpful) | |
|---|---|
| | • Minimum of eight years experience working in a generalist role, with at least 5 years working in a manufacturing environment. Experience managing multiple locations is strongly preferred. Preference for # of locations?<br><br>• Experience in operational environment who can relate to factory floor and operational employees. Retail/restaurant experience could work.<br><br>• Union experience a plus What in the environment makes this a plus?<br><br>• Bachelor's degree in Human Resources or related field Masters degree preferred.<br><br>Coaching experience<br>Drive strategies, efficiencies,<br>Leadership experience in a lean environment |

## Now You Get to Play

1.   Put your job description into the launch document

2.   Mark in red areas that are vague, as well as any questions you have about what is in the job description

3.   Add additional questions you want to ask

4.   Highlight the questions on the launch document. If it's easier for you, delete the ones you know you won't want to ask.

5.   Enjoy your launch meeting or phone call with the hiring manager. You are about to have your best search ever!

Oh, Wait! One last thing: The more detail you can get about the position, the easier it is going to be for you to create a compelling job posting that will pull the most qualified candidates to apply for your position.

Be sure to read the next bonus report *Creating Magnetic Postings* for the process of taking what you hear in the launch meeting to create a fabulous posting your ideal candidates won't be able to resist.

Below is one of my most prized possessions, my launch document, and it's in the forms document that accompanies The Consultative Recruiter ebook. That version is in word format so you can modify it to fit every situation.

I started this document at the very beginning of my recruiting career and have carried it with me to every job and search I've had since. It's a little like the sour dough starter the miners carried to California during the gold rush!

I've filled many different kinds of positions at salaries from $35,000 annually to over a million dollars in a wide variety of companies. This launch document and process have been critical to my success in every situation.

I hope you have a fabulous time with your launch meetings. I know your hiring managers will really be impressed and appreciative. And you will have your best search ever.

**Comprehensive Search Launch Document**

| POSITION PROFILE | |
|---|---|
| Position Title: | Compensation: |
| | Base |
| Location: | Bonus |
| | Other |
| # of openings: | Exempt: Yes __ No__ |
| | |
| Hiring Manager: | Hiring Manager's Title: |
| Hiring Manager Email: | Preferred communication method: |
| Hiring Manager Phone: | |
| HR Business Partner: | HRBP Preferred Communication method: |
| __ New Position | Name of Previous Employee: |
| __ Replacement | Terminated ___ Resigned ___ |
| Travel %: ____ | |
| Travel to where: | For what purposes: |
| Will considering relocating a candidate __Yes __ No | |
| Relocation assistance available? __Yes __ No | |
| | |

| INTERNAL/EXTERNAL FACTORS | |
|---|---|
| ☐ Internal candidates only  ☐External candidates only  ☐ Internal and External candidates | |
| Additional info about why this position is available: Is this a newly defined position? Is it open as a result of business growth/redirection? Did the previous person get promoted? | |
| Background/qualifications of predecessor What was missing? | |
| Success factors of predecessor or the best people in the position. | |
| What do/did they do that was better than expected? | |
| What traits would the hiring manager like to have replicated in the new person? | |

| POSITION DETAILS | |
|---|---|
| Position Overview | |
| Responsibilities and job duties | |

129

| | |
|---|---|
| Experience and background of the ideal candidate (required, desired, helpful) | |
| Job objectives to be achieved within first 90 days, 6 months, first year—whatever is the first evaluation point. Which is the most important; what makes it the most important? | |
| What is the most important task for this position? What makes it important to you? | |
| What are the key issues this person would need to address short-term? Longer-term? Internal and external? | |
| Key challenges to be met in this role | |
| Any challenges to success? Internal? External? | |
| How does this position fit into the long-term strategic goals for the organization? | |
| Competencies (softer skills, e.g., leadership, team player, self-motivated, etc.) | |
| What makes this a great career opportunity? | |
| What makes it exciting to the types of candidates you are looking to attract? | |
| Career growth potential (either promotionally, acquiring new skills, etc.) | |

## THE TEAM

| | |
|---|---|
| If there is someone on the team who feels this position should be theirs, are they a viable candidate? If not, what are they missing that makes them not a fit for the role | |
| Does this position manage a team and/or supervisor others? | |
| If so, what titles report to the position? How many of each? | |
| How many people are on this team? | |
| What titles/jobs are a part of this team? | |
| What are the dynamics of the team? What is the culture of the team? | |
| Is the team fully functional and performing at the level you want them to reach? | |

## THE TEAM

| Are there issues with the team, e.g., morale, need to replacement, training, performance, etc.? | |
| --- | --- |
| Will there be a need to increase the team in the short term? | |
| How many years of experience of management would you like to see this person have? | |

## THE COMPANY, CULTURE AND MANAGER

| What is happening in the company overall, this portion of the company, this department, etc., that would be important and/or interesting for the candidate to know? | |
| --- | --- |
| What does the near term future look like? What new things are you planning? What are you excited about in your business? | |
| How would you describe the culture today? What is it like to work in this group? | |
| What are you like to work for? What is your personal style, preferred management style, etc.? | |
| For relatively new managers, what specifically made you join the company? What are you most enjoying about the company and your role? | |
| | |

## SOURCING

| Has the hiring manager asked their employees for referrals? Employee referral program? | |
| --- | --- |
| Target Companies (competitions, parallel industries, end users) | |
| Companies not of interest (because of their culture, business practices, etc., that would make employees incompatible with us) | |
| Are there companies with whom there are strategic partnerships, vendor relationships, etc., that would make it inappropriate for us to hire someone from that company? | |
| Will the hiring manager post on their own LinkedIn, do they have any referrals networks, etc. | |
| What associations does the hiring manager belong to that would include potential candidates for this role? | |

## PRE-SCREENING INFORMATION

| | |
|---|---|
| Are there 3 – 5 key questions you would like me to ask candidates as a part of our screening process? (Be sure to ask them for the components of a good answer. You may know the answer, but it's important to hear it from the hiring manager.) | 1.<br><br>2.<br><br>3. |
| What is one question that you would like me to ask in the phone interview and what would be a great answer to look for? | |
| Are there key categories of people you are looking for (e.g., hard charger, creative, intellectually curious, etc.)? | |
| If so, how do you define those terms? | |
| How do you know when you're sitting across from a great candidate? | |
| If I handed you a resume what would be on it that would make this the ideal candidate for this role? | |
| If the first candidate you meet is a really good fit and meets your qualifications, would you be willing to move forward with an offer?<br><br>If they say no, or say "yes" but don't seem to really mean it, ask: How many candidates do you feel you would like to see in order to know you've seen the best of those who expressed interest? | If the hiring manager is prone to wanting to see a lot of candidates: |
| If they have outrageous expectations, this is where you can start to talk about the realities of the market place—competitors, how many candidates will actually meet all the requirements, etc.<br><br>Then consider saying something like: Let's go to market with this position and see how many qualified candidates raise their hand and express interest. In a week or so, we'll know what the candidate flow looks like and can see how to move forward so we get a great candidate while adhering as much as possible to your urgency to fill. Would that work for you? | |
| When would it be ideal for you to have the position filled? (You probably know the answer to this. But by asking, you now have the manager's words around their sense of urgency. If during the search they aren't behaving in accordance with the urgency they expressed in the launch meeting, you can ask non-confrontational questions about whether things have changed, are there other ways to keep the candidate moving so "we can meet your desired timeframe for filling this position.") | If the HM sometimes seems to lose the requisite sense of urgency, ask this in the launch meeting so you can deal with this when/if it happens during the search.<br><br>Also check out Strategy Technique #1 to get things back on track without having to be confrontational. |

## Resume Review Process

| | |
|---|---|
| How does the hiring manager want to receive resumes for review, e.g., one at a time via email, once a week in a phone call or meeting with you, when you have a certain number ready for review, etc.? | |
| If the hiring manager has been slow getting you the necessary feedback in the past, ask what would make that step easier for them. How soon, on average, will the hiring manager get back to you on resumes? | |
| See Appendix A:<br><br>Rather than tell them to get back to you within X hours, use the Commitment Technique so they make the decision. It makes all the difference. | |

## INTERVIEW STRUCTURE

| | | | | |
|---|---|---|---|---|
| ☐ Round 1 Interview | ☐ Phone<br>Interviewer(s): | ☐ Individual | ☐ Panel | Targeted #: |
| ☐ Round 2 Interview | ☐ Phone<br>Interviewer (s): | ☐ Individual | ☐ Panel | Targeted #: |
| ☐ Round 3 Interview | ☐ Phone<br>Interviewer(s): | ☐ Individual | ☐ Panel | Targeted #: |

| | |
|---|---|
| Who else needs to be included in the interview process? If they are not available, do you need to wait for them, is there an alternative person or will you just leave them out this time?<br><br>Does everyone involved in the interview process understand the position, what is important to be accomplished in the role, experience required, etc.? Have they seen and/or had input into the posting?<br><br>Are you asking certain people to interview for certain experiences, qualities, etc., of the candidate? Do the interviewers know your expectations of what they will be looking for?<br><br>What is the biggest benefit you get as the hiring manager from having these people involved in the interview process? | If the hiring manager wants lots of people to interview your candidates, use these questions to learn about the reasons for that approach.<br><br>To influence behavior, you first need to know what motivates it. This conversation alone may not be sufficient to get the changes you would like right now.<br><br>But it starts the conversation that will allow you to have more influence on this topic throughout the search. |
| After each interview, when do you think you will be able to provide feedback and outline next steps, if any, for the candidate? | |
| What will be the first step in the process? Will you want us to meet the candidate before you meet them? | |
| If you like the candidate, what are the next steps? Who interviews at each step? | |

| | |
|---|---|
| Will you want to try to have all candidates to interview on the same day? How will that day be structured? | |
| If holding candidates already in process to find sufficient number of candidates to form a slate is not feasible, are you flexible on moving people through the process rather than hold everyone until a slate is created? | |
| How long does the typical process take from first interview to offer decision? Is that your ideal timeframe? | |
| How many candidates do you typically move to 2$^{nd}$ and beyond interviews before choosing a finalist and making an offer? | |
| Are things like preparing a 90-day business plan, giving a presentation, etc., part of your process? | |
| Have you shared your desired timeline and expectations of the role they will play with everyone? | |
| Does everyone involved in the interview process understand the position, what is important to be accomplished in the role, experience required, etc.? Have they seen and/or had input into the posting? | |
| Are you asking certain people to interview for certain experiences, qualities, etc., of the candidate? Do the interviewers know your expectations of what they will be looking for? | |
| Does everyone involved in the interview process have a vote? Who gets a vote and who just gets to have an opinion? Do they know? | |
| How do you collect feedback from the other interviewers? | |

# Bonus Report 3: How to Create Irresistible Job Postings

## In a Nutshell: Why This Matters

Simply because of these two realities:

1. Job descriptions serve some corporate purposes, but they aren't written for candidates.

   If we were sitting in comfy rocking chairs on a shaded veranda on a warm summer afternoon and drinking tall drinks with umbrellas and maybe some fruit in them, we would probably admit that job descriptions are useless for recruiting purposes.

   The main reason is that they are vague, use wording that seems to make sense until you read it one more time, and often are outdated for the world today. It's like we all made some tacit agreement to pretend we know what job they are describing, but even without those drinks, we would also probably admit that job descriptions make really really really bad postings.

   They give the candidate almost no idea of what they would be doing, what makes it a great career opportunity, etc. The candidate has to fill in all those blanks, and if you or your hiring manager think they will do that, read 2) below.

2. People (candidates, hiring managers and everyone else) process information differently and faster than ever—a Twitter and other social media heritage, etc. So if you don't capture their interest and keep it long enough for them to get the idea of your position, you're toast. If something is unclear, confusing, or long and looks old-school, people will leave.

   Think of it this way: **If you confuse them, you lose them.**

## What You Get by Creating Captivating Job Postings

1. More and better qualified candidates
2. Faster times to fill your positions
3. Happier hiring managers

## Guidelines for Creating Irresistible Job Postings

- Make the ideal candidate feel as though you are talking to them as they read your posting
- Be specific about what the job entails that is important to the ideal candidate, e.g., what is it about this kind of work that makes your ideal candidate say "This is why I do this job."?
- Answer the questions you know they will ask. The reason this helps is that if people have questions, they are more likely to click away and just move on. Plus, when you answer the most important and most frequently-asked questions in your posting, you won't have to answer them over and over in your phone screening calls!
- Explain what makes the position important to the company, to clients, to the other employees, etc.

- Add some passion about what makes it great. If there is excitement conveyed in your posting, your ideal candidates will be captivated. If you as the recruiter are excited about the position based on what you learned and wrote about it, that excitement seems to get conveyed to your best candidates.

## Standing out is a good thing—and essential!

- Unexpected subject line or heading will make your posting stand out from others. Check postings for jobs with the same title on indeed.com and linkedin.com and you'll see what the competition is saying. Say something that will appeal to what your ideal candidates would love to find in a position. See Sound Bites & Headlines examples below.

- If the title your company uses is not the typical title, use the typical title in the heading. Then in the body of the posting you can mention that in your company this position has the title of ___. Sometimes it's tempting to just go with the internal title and not deal with this issue. But if you follow the next two steps, I know you will be happy you did!

  Sometimes this kind of change gives your hiring manager, HRBP and/or compensation committee the jitters. A good way to help the hiring manager et al to understand the importance of this modification is to give them some statistics. When I start a search with a title I haven't heard before, I check LinkedIn to see how many people have that title TODAY.

  If that number is too small, do a search for the title you feel is probably more traditional. If that number is larger, now you have the data that demonstrates to all involved parties in your company why you are using the more commonly-used position title *for posting purposes only*.

- The more you tell the more believable it seems. Actually there is research that supports this. Apparently when a detailed description is next to a short vague description, the longer more, detailed information is seen as more credible. So the more you include in the posting, the more believable it seems. Plus it looks very different. So tell people what you would say if you had them on the phone and wanted them to be excited about the position.

  See examples below that will guide you and free you from that boring old fluffy job description. People may say it's good, but it's not a good posting. It's probably not even a good description of the position, but since we're not using it, that doesn't matter anymore.

## Quick Tips for Actually Writing the Posting

### Just 30 minutes

Plan to spend about 30 minutes to get to your first really good draft. Don't think you need to take a week end or work late into the night. Not at all because you actually already have most of the posting done. It's just that it's in your head, and we just need to get it on paper/screen.

### Create A Structure

Decide on the sections, e.g., position overview, responsibilities, 6 months accomplishments, background required, company info, culture info, what makes it a great opportunity.

These sections can be moved around in the posting, combined with another component, or even omitted as appropriate for your ideal candidates. But once you have the sections that you would probably include in ALL postings, writing the posting will get easier and faster (and better) every time you create one.

For example, adding info about what makes it a great opportunity might be a good first paragraph in the position overview, especially for difficult to fill positions. Where there is competition for positions, a bit of info about the company that talks about what is exciting that people might not realize could be a good opening.

### Get Ready to Write

If you did a launch meeting with the Hiring Manger, put your notes from that into the appropriate sections so you only have to work with one document. That speeds things up, and makes sure you get the good stuff you heard from the hiring manager. It is easier to write a really exciting posting when you have all the information in one place, and did I mention "faster"?

Now that you've had a chance to review and categorize what you know about the position, think about what stands out, what makes the position intriguing, what image(s) really let the ideal candidates see themselves in the position, what did the hiring manager say that makes a great sound bite.

### What to Say

Think about what you would say to a candidate you really wanted to interest in the position. Now write those things down.

If you had the ideal candidate on the phone, what would you tell them first, second, third? Focus on sharing metaphors and images of "life in the role" make your positions memorable and truly differentiate them from the competition. What images would you share with them?

Now you can move them around into a nice flow, but again, do it quickly. Use a tone and language that reflects your company's culture. If you're casual and fast moving, communicate that way. If it's a more intellectual and formal environment, you probably have learned to write that way, so be sure to do that in the posting.

Don't worry about grammar, making it sound "professional" or fancy. Write it the way you would say it.

Most important of all: Write it as if you were talking to an ideal candidate.

### Examples:

- Come share a Route 44® Shake from the Sonic Drive-in with us as we decompress every so often—sitting on the exercise ball will be optional.
- Everyone at Children's is totally and completely focused on making kids better. Everyone agrees: when all you do is help kids get better, something wonderful happens--they make you better.
- SusieCakes' Founder and CEO, Susan Sarich baked with her grandmothers, who called her Susie, every day after school. She carried her grandmothers' carefully recorded recipes on handwritten 4x6 cards when she moved to Brentwood and opened her first SusieCakes Bakery with treats based on those "with love" recipes.
- Lots of companies say they care about the communities they serve. Without judging the reasons for getting a tattoo, Providence (Healthcare System) recognizes that it is a decision that can result in biased judgments, denied employment or becoming the victim of violence. Removing a tattoo can be life changing, but very

expensive. The Providence tattoo removal clinics offer individuals a chance to make a positive life change by removing their tattoo and accepting community service hours in exchange for payments.

- Love shoes? Thank World Shoe Company for bringing them to you. World Shoe Association is the largest footwear trade market in The Americas. The twice-yearly show at the Mandalay Bay Convention Center and Sands Expo in Las Vegas, Nevada, pulls in more than 35,000 participants and the cream of the footwear manufacturing industry. It's where the decisions are made what shoes you'll see in your favorite stores.

## Sound Bites & Headlines

### Creating Excitement at First Glance

These came directly from the hiring managers and became great sound bites for the posting heading, as well as often being the perfect subject line for the LinkedIn Recruiter Inmail:

### Examples

- General Manager & Master business builder with the 2400 mile smile, (GM of division 2400 miles from Corp HQ)
- Opportunity to build the kind of sales function you've always wanted to lead, (VP Business Development for a professional services firm)
- Contract Recruiter: We need you to organize, strategize and help us herd the cats, (Contract Recruiter)
- eBay Head of Fashion Vertical: Key role in determining the on-line fashion experience for the next decade, The Designer role you've waited for if design is in your genes (for a jeans retailer),
- SVP/CFO for a complex organization focused on making children feel better. (SVP/CFO for Children's Hospital)
- opportunity to create the playbook while playing the game at a very high level (Addressable Video Digital Product Manager)

## Fill in the Blanks Template

1. In this *(new, newly defined, expanded, etc., if one of those is appropriate. Remember that at some time you have to explain what is happening to require a new position be created, or what it means that it has been newly defined or expanded, why the position is open, etc.)* _____ position

2. Reporting to _____ *(this lets candidates know where they fit in the organizational structure and can cut down on applications from under- and over-qualified candidates.)*

3. You will work primarily _____. *(Here you can put kinds of people this position interacts with, numbers of offices, types of clients, etc., and the primary responsibility for this role. Include what you know will be of interest to your ideal candidate so they keep reading. If the opening )*

Sample: *Reporting to the Regional Vice President-Sales-Northeast, the Sales Client Manager will work in the Boston, MA, office, supporting 15 business development executives as well as managing sales activities for approximately 45 assigned client accounts, helping everyone keep all kinds of essential projects on schedule.*

4. Location: Identify city (and state if appropriate) as in sample above if there will be any question. If you have multiple offices in a city, add "located in our Charleston Street office" type of information. If you can relocate a candidate, add a brief statement about a relocation package being or not being available. Then candidates willing to make a move for your position know you're open to non-local candidates

5. Details: Provide what you know the candidates will wonder about. If you are sourcing passive candidates, they know the details of their current job. If you want to get them to consider your job, let them feel they know at least some of what they will be doing. A long list of bullets under "Responsibilities" won't do this. And people tend to only skim long lists of bullets anyway.

    a. Information about the team this person will join or manage, how many people, whether team is located virtually, whether team needs to be increased, etc.

    b. # of projects managed, clients managed, sales execs supported, etc.

    c. A detailed description of some of what they might be doing in a typical day, e.g., types of projects, software to be implemented, number of customers supported and types of problems resolved, types of communications to be developed, etc.

4. What else they will get to do/learn/etc. based on what you know is important to these candidates or what will your ideal candidate think is really cool about the opportunity.

5. What makes this important to the organization?

6. What does your ideal candidate love about doing their work? If it's true, let them know they would get to do that in this role.

## 2 Typical FAQs

**Q: Should I worry about the length? The posting turns out to be very different than the job description, and my hiring manager is not big on doing things differently.**

**A:** Sometimes people (especially your hiring manager, for example) will express concern about the longer length and a posting that looks different than what people are used to. Let them know that, in addition to the research mentioned above, this longer length is a response to how people process information and how they read web data today.

This more complete posting you've written is a reflection of your strategy to captivate and engage the very best candidates. You may want to have a brief conversation with your hiring manager to talk about how you are addressing the reality of how people process information today and how important it is to have a captivating posting.

Share with your hiring manager how many similar positions are available based on postings on LinkedIn and/or Indeed.com. This is even more evidence that it is critical that your posting speaks to the candidates the hiring manager wants to see, because you probably have some considerable competition for candidates for the role.

So when you include a more comprehensive description, it's more likely your great candidates will find what they are looking for! Plus, I've never heard an interested candidate complain that there was too much information. At the same time no one has ever said they would have applied if only the posting hadn't been so long!

Interested target candidates will want to know as much as possible. They will want to read enough great information to warrant them taking action—applying for your position. So you are increasing the odds that your posting has the information that will move them to action.

**Q:** Are there any guidelines for formatting the posting for how people read what's on their screens?

**A:** Yes, in consideration of the fact almost everyone will be reading your posting on their laptop, iPad, mobile devices, etc., you need to violate some traditional writing rules. Finally, you have permission to ignore the rules!

• Shorter sentences are easier to read than longer sentences.

- Each paragraph should be only 2-3 sentences. I know that isn't what you learned in High School English, but it is essential if you want people to read your posting.
- Use bullets to list items, of course. But don't do long lists with bullets. A list over 5-6 bullets will probably get skimmed and not read. So bullet the most important things.
- Feel free to leave off some of the usual items in the job description. For most positions, it's probably not necessary to list computer skills as a requirement. At the same time, if the position requires a valid driver's license, that is important to be listed.
- If you have 3-4 bullet points that are important, consider putting them into a brief paragraph in the position description. That really increases the likelihood they will actually be read. Remember, once people get to the bullets, they skim and skip.
- Be sure to check your posting on your cell phone. Current research indicates 50% or more of your candidates are going to read your posting on their cells. As you know, if it's difficult for them to get the information they are looking for, or to take the next step in your process, they will skip your position and move on to the next. If you're sourcing passive candidates, this is even more important.

# The Consultative Recruiter

## 5 Hacks
## Cheat Sheets

### Resolve Your
### Five Biggest
### Time-Wasting Situations

Katherine Moody

TheConsultativeRecruiter.com

# Bonus Report 4: Cheat Sheets to Solve Your 5 Most Frustrating, Time Wasting Recruiting Situations

## # 1 Situation: Delayed Feedback

**Tell me what you're thinking:** HM does not get back to you with feedback about resumes, interviews, etc. Despite your frequent follow up, they do not respond as they promised.

## Solution

It is certainly understandable that you would be trying everything possible to get their feedback, including sending lots of emails, making lots of phone calls, etc. The problem is that trying to follow up that way just reinforces an order taker image.

PLUS: it takes a long time to get your HM to respond because you know you have to keep reminding them.

It's also not good for your image to just finally go to their door (or their supervisor or the HRBP) as a last ditch effort to get feedback. It may work this time, but you've just taught your HM that they can continue to ignore your requests for their feedback because when you're desperate enough, you'll come to them.

This is one of those nearly invisible situations (below the water line on the recruiter iceberg) that adds to your work and wastes your time because:

- You have to keep contacting candidates to keep them interested
- You spend time trying to track down your HM

So not only does this drive you crazy and add to your work load, your time to fill metrics just keep getting longer.

If your company has an SLA, you may wonder if it's appropriate for you to take action or if you should just wait for them to start following what you thought they agreed to do in the SLA. If that hasn't happened yet, it probably isn't going to. You need to do something new.

Use the "Give me a commitment" technique outlined word for word below.

After the HM makes a commitment to you, they may not keep that commitment. Well, we're prepared to deal with that without resorting to that old order taker behavior.

If they don't keep to their commitment, about 10 minutes after the time agreed upon has past, ask the second question in the technique. You don't have to wait. Take action by taking the second step in the technique.

It may seem like it would be faster if you could just tell them when you need the information and they delivered it at that time.

Of course the truth is that it would be faster **but only if telling them really worked.**

**Results you can expect when you use this technique:**

Not only will you get the information you need faster and with less work on your part, doing this positions you as a business partner and trusted advisor.

Taking this approach rather than continually chasing your HMs is probably one of the most impactful changes you can make in your relationship with them.

Using the Commitment technique means you will fill positions faster! That results in happier HMs, HRBPs and your manager.

**TIP:** Don't keep contacting the HM to get feedback.

Take action immediately if they miss the deadline. Take action every time they miss a deadline. Don't worry. They will get the message that you expect they will live up to their commitments.

Ask the Commitment technique questions live or on the phone. Don't try to do this through email, and at the same time, don't think this will only work if you are meeting them face to face.

| How to Get a Real Commitment Without Chasing Them |
|---|
| **The secret to getting a commitment:** Let your hiring manager make the decision. When you tell them when you need them to get back to you in such and such a timeframe, they may say OK, but that's not a commitment. |
| **The secret to success with this**: Don't say anything until they answer your question—no options, no explanations (unless they ask), no filling in the silence while they think, etc. It will be tempting to jump in, but resist. |

| Getting an Initial Commitment | Handling a Missed Commitment |
|---|---|
| Ask the hiring manager: "<br>• *When do you think you will be able to get back to me with …*<br>fill in the blank: feedback on resumes, candidate interviews, decision re hiring, etc.<br><br>Don't talk about needing to move quickly, losing candidates, etc. They get it even though they may not act as though they do. | • *"When we talked you thought it would work for you to get back to me in X (days, hours, etc.). That doesn't seem to work for you. What would be better for you?"*<br><br>Be sure not to sound snarky or PO'd when you ask (even though I would understand if you feel that way!) And ask this question right after they miss the commitment deadline they had originally chosen.. |
| <br><br>**Now the hard part:**<br>**Don't say anything else until they answer you.**<br>Let them make the decision because that's how you get a commitment.<br>Lather, Rinse, Repeat | <br><br>**Now the hard part:**<br>**Don't say anything else until they answer you.**<br>Let them make the decision because that's how you get a commitment.<br>Lather, Rinse, Repeat |

# No Sense of Urgency?

**When the HM doesn't seem to have a sense of urgency, you get to take ....A Soft Pause**

When you start a search or at least before submitting candidates, determine how quickly the HM wants the position filled. **Ask this question** (even if you know what they are going to say):

- *When would it be ideal to have this filled?*

**And of course, now the hard part: Don't say anything else until they answer you.**
**Later,** when the HM wants to take a long time before they get back to you:
You say:

"When we talked, you were thinking you wanted to fill this as quickly as possible. But if that timeframe is not relevant any more, no problem. I'll just go on a soft pause until you have a chance to get me the feedback that lets me know what the next steps should be.

Of course, if someone great shows up, I'll certainly bring them to you, but in the meantime, I'll just go on soft pause."

Now you have to do two hard things: **Don't say anything else until they answer you AND don't do a lecture about urgency. That is not the route to influence and it won't get you any good results.**

# # 2 Situation: Not a Fit

**Not a fit.** HMs give vague feedback on candidates. They say things like "Didn't blow my socks off," "Just don't think they will be a fit."

# Solution

One reason HMs may not give you the important details is because they really don't know how to express those details. Just because they have the title "hiring manager" doesn't mean they are good as interviewing and evaluating candidates. That is often the reason your HM may use the same vague phrases over and over, and why they often rely on *feelings* based feedback.

That means they are hoping to have a good feeling as a way to know when they are looking at the right candidate.

Of course, it's also possible they are just busy and think they don't have time to slow down to give you details.

So no matter what the reason, here is how to get the information that will help you, while continuing to build your relationship with your HM.

The key in this situation is to ask detailed questions. The more you learn about the specifics of their thinking, the faster and easier it will be to fill the position. You will really be helping the hiring manager when you ask questions that help them think through their decision.

NOTE: you must come from a sense of curiosity, no frustration or exasperation with your HM. If you are truly interested, the HM will be more willing to spend a little time answering your questions.

It may seem like a slower approach, and in a way it is! But with a little patience and some good questions, you will get exactly what you need so you know how to move the search forward.

You have to slow down just a bit, and break down your questions so they are very granular, and be willing to ask for more information or for them to expand on their answer. You cannot ask what I call "big picture" questions because your HM won't be able to answer them.

Big questions like "What didn't you like?" or "Why are you deciding to pass on the candidate?" won't get you useful information…if it gets you any response at all.

**Ask questions like:**

- *What would it take to have you see the candidate(s) as a fit, blow your socks off, etc. Use the phrase they used.*
- *Was there a particular question the candidate answered incorrectly?*
- *Did they do something during the interview that made you come to that conclusion?*
- *Can you give me an idea of what is missing in the candidate's experience, personality, fit potential, etc.?*
- *How did you feel the candidate stacked up against the requirements? (You may have to list each requirement to get a sense of how the HM/HRBP evaluated the candidate. if you ask a question like "Do you think they fit the requirements?" it's probably too difficult for them to answer in a way that helps you.*
- *How do you know when you're sitting across from a great candidate?*
- *What is the one thing you really hope to find in a candidate, or hear them say?*

These questions will help the HM give you feedback that is real and useful feedback. This is how you help them go beyond "not a fit."

**TIP:** When HMs/HRBPs say things like "not a fit" or "don't think I will move them forward", don't respond with OK and then just go away without asking any clarifying questions.

If you don't have more information, you are just going to have to work harder, maybe longer hours, but you don't really know what they want. This is a no-win position for you! Let's change that!

## #3 Situation: Send Me More!

**Send me more.** HM wants to see more and more candidates, even though the ones you've sent so far meet the requirements. Sometimes it seems like the HM either isn't sure about what they need or they keep adding requirements, often based on the most recent resume or candidate they saw.

## Solution

Even if you think you know the answer, it's helpful to explore at the beginning of a search how many candidates the HM needs to see before making a decision. Sometimes we don't ask this question because we're afraid of what the answer might be.

However, you might as well ask the question because they probably have some number in mind. They usually don't think to tell you that number until much later in the search. No matter how perfect the candidate they hire is, they will often feel uncomfortable (meaning "unhappy with you") if they didn't get to see whatever number they have been thinking of as "enough".

**Ask this question:**

- *If the first candidate you interview is a good fit and meets the requirements, would you be willing to make an offer?*

If your HM hesitates or says NO, **ask this question:**

- *Do you have a particular number of candidates you feel you need to see before you can make a decision?*

Usually the number will be realistic. If it seems high (and 7+ is starting to get too high for most positions, to me at least) explore the reasons they feel they would like to see that many. Avoid the "too much time will be wasted" or "we'll never find that many qualified candidates" lectures.

You won't be able to address their concerns and move them to a more realistic number if you don't know what they are really thinking. Don't push back here; rather be interested.

**Ask this question:**

- *I would be interested in your thoughts about what would be the reason to see that number? What information would interviewing that many candidates provide you that would be helpful in making your hiring decision?*

(Please avoid asking any question that starts with **why** because those questions can make the HM defensive. And you don't get the best response.)

If the numbers requirement is met and still no hiring decision, you can help the HM here also.

**Ask these questions:** Even if you've asked some of these before, good to ask again.

- *Are you thinking you just need to see more people like the ones you've seen or do you want to see candidates with a different skill set or experience?*
- *What new skills/experiences do you want to see?*
- *Do you have a particular number of candidates you feel you need to see before you can make a decision?*
- *Can you take me through all the things you would like to see in the additional candidates that you aren't seeing so far?*
- *Have you seen anyone so far that you would like to move forward to the next steps?*

If the HM seems to be waffling, or perhaps mixing up the candidates and how the meet the requirements, you can be a big help here. Create a grid with ALL the requirements, plus all the feedback items you've heard from the HM throughout the search, no matter how small or off the wall.

Put each candidate in a separate column and indicate which qualifications the candidate meets, and discuss the results with your HM. Or perhaps do the grid comparison with your HM. This is a good way to make sure you and the HM are on the same page. Plus it helps your HM see the real picture of the candidates in process.

Plus there is a real impact to be able to see a visual evaluation of each candidate compared to the requirements and each other.

**TIP:**

Here again, resist saying "OK" and then going away hoping you'll be able to get a hiring decision if you just keep sending in more candidates. Eventually you will get a hire, but it will take a lot of extra and probably unnecessary work on your part. And it blows your "time to fill" metric out of the water.

## #4 Situation: Doesn't Everyone Wants to Work for Us?

**Surely everyone wants to work for us.** Managers often think your company is the cutest baby on the block, so you won't have any trouble recruiting for their position. This means they think they will be seeing lots of highly qualified (and even over qualified) candidates in just a few days.

Also, they may be unaware of the recruiting challenges you're facing such as, how generational differences impact the recruiting for their positions, how people view your company, the competitive landscape which means good candidates have lots of opportunities to join great companies, and finally that those great companies may be paying as much/more as your company, offering higher level titles, etc.

## Solution

When you approach dealing with this situation from the perspective of **"I'd be interested in your thoughts"** approach, you can help your HM begin to gain an understanding of market realities, without making them feel foolish. Have this conversation as early in the process as possible, ideally at the meeting where you launch.

Even if you are already working and on the search and didn't get to ask these questions at the beginning of your efforts, NOW is always a good time.

When sharing market data, preface it with something like "This is what we are hearing/seeing in the market place from the kinds of candidates you would want…"

Remember, share, don't lecture. If you just dump a lot of data on them, even if it's n a pretty graphic or PowerPoint, they can/will tune it and you out. Make it a conversation.

**Ask these questions:** Even if you think you know the answers. This is the best way to get the HM thinking beyond "Everyone will want to work for us."

- *What makes this a great opportunity?*

Let them tell you how they see it. You may be surprised at how little they have to say at this point. Now you can talk about the things you know will make great candidates excited. You can also compare those things to what candidates might find at other companies.

- *If you were sitting across from a great candidate, what would you tell them makes this a great career opportunity?*
- *How do you feel our opportunity compares to (great companies looking to hire the same candidates you are)? You probably will hear a lot of misinformation that you can start to change in this conversation.*
- *If we are going to pay less than what people in this position are already making, what would you say to convince a candidate that taking a pay cut to work with us would be a good career move?*
- *Would you be willing to look at candidates who fit your requirements if they are making 10-20% more?*

- *Would you be willing to look at candidates in your compensation range if they don't have quite all the requirements? Which requirements could we be flexible on?*

These questions will give you a lot of good information about what your HM is thinking. At the same time, they are non-confrontational ways to get the HM to begin to realize what they are looking for may not exist, may not fit your compensation range, may have equally attractive opportunities at other great companies, etc.

If the HM says or acts like it's your job to answer these questions, agree with them. Also point out that, ultimately, it will be what candidates hear from the HM that plays a major role in their decision to join or not join your company.

Make it clear you will be doing absolutely everything possible to get the best candidates within the desired comp range, meeting all the requirements, etc., to be interested enough to raise their hand to be considered. At the same time, you will bring them candidates who could do a great job even if they are slightly over the comp range or are a little light on some experience. If your HM is ok with this, you are on the right track to get your HM back on track!

If you are having a discussion you've had before, recognize that it may be falling on deaf ears, or even feel like a lecture which they will tune out. Here is how to break through to them. As you talk, **every so often ask questions like:**

- *Does that make sense?*
- *Would you agree?*
- *What do you think?*

This gets people into the rhythm of saying "yes" to your ideas. Plus it subtly moves them into alignment with what you are saying. If they don't agree (or aren't even listening) NOW is the time to find out so you can get them back on the same page with you.

## #5 Situation: Last Minute Surprises

You find out the HM and their boss and/or other key decision makers do not agree on what they are looking for.

So late in the process, just when you're thinking the position is about to be filled, you are most likely starting over.

## Solution

While these situations will complicate your life when they happen, they are also fabulous opportunities to demonstrate your consultative expertise. It may seem like the HM should do this, or perhaps it hasn't been something you have done before. Frankly, you may be **the only one** who can help them bridge the gaps and avoid delays in getting their positions filled.

First, even though you are understandably upset, avoid the impulse to lecture them about things like "How come we didn't know this sooner?"

Here is how to have the conversation that closes the gap. If you know from experience that one or more of these issues exist, try to have the conversation when you have the first discussion about the position. If it's later in the process before you get that last minute surprise, have the conversation as soon as you learn about it. NOW is always the best time.

Ideally, you will have a launch meeting that includes the people who have veto power or their approval is needed. These questions are also effective when you have HMs who want lots of people to interview their candidates. **Ask these questions:**

- *Who in addition to you will be a part of the hiring decision?*
- *Will they have veto power or will you just be soliciting their input for your decision?*
- *Even if they don't have veto power, is there anyone you really want to agree with your hiring decision? How does that person impact you or the candidate in the job?*
- *So we will want to make sure everyone is on the same page and you all agree on what constitutes a great candidate, and the experience and style you all want in this position. So perhaps we should include the most important decision makers in the launch meeting. That way you can hear what the other person thinks is important, and we'll all be on the same page throughout the entire search. Would it be ok with you to include them in that meeting?*

If the HM doesn't want to have their boss or other people in that meeting, **ask these questions:**

- *What are you thinking would be the downside of that approach?*
- *What about if I just let the other decision maker(s) know what you and I discussed?*
- *We probably want everyone on the same page from the beginning. Would that help you? Would that be OK?*

If the HM objects, you need to ask questions that uncover their thinking. It isn't a good idea to lecture them about the reason other people should be in the meeting, etc.

Keep going with these questions of curiosity to understand their thinking and move them to agreement to getting everyone in agreement before you start sourcing candidates. If you wait any longer, you run the real risk of decisions that will delay closing the position and possibly send you back to find more candidates.

If you found out about the situation late in the game, e.g., candidates the HM liked got nixed by someone else, you have to take control. Have a conversation like the one below. You can be flexible, but stick to your goal to get everyone on the same page NOW.

*Perhaps it would work for us to have a brief meeting or conference call with the key players to set out what you are looking for in a candidate to make sure they understand and agree. What do you think? We need to know what they are thinking also, don't you think?*

OR

*It would be interesting to have more details about why the other person(s) didn't like the candidate you liked. I would like to get together with the two of you to learn more about their thinking. What do you think?*

It may seem like this is far from taking control. Wouldn't it be wonderful if you could just tell people what to do and they would do it? But if that hasn't worked so far, we need a different strategy. And the worst strategy of all? Not doing anything, hoping that next time something will be different.

# QUICK START CHECKLIST

| If your situation is… | Perspective | Use these techniques… | Use these tools… |
|---|---|---|---|
| Hiring managers don't seem to take recruiting as seriously as you feel they should. | As you begin to execute the strategy for creating a partnership relationship with your hiring managers, they will respond with a sense of accountability and ownership of their parts of the recruiting process. It doesn't happen overnight, but with these techniques, it will happen. | 1, 2, 3, 4, 12 | Comprehensive launch document will help get HM engaged |
| Hiring managers don't seem to be happy with the recruiting function. | From the beginning of a search, you can structure a process that sets forth expectations on both sides. Plus learn how to deal positively and effectively in those situations where you or the hiring manager doesn't meet those expectations. | 3, 11, 12 | |
| Hiring managers don't follow the "process". | It's just not possible to "mandate" that people follow a process. You can guide your hiring managers in a way that will make it easier for them to follow the process one step at a time. | 7 | Strategy Sheet #1 |
| Hiring managers are frustrated with time the search takes | One of the key metrics used almost everywhere almost insures hiring managers will be frustrated with the length of a search. Learn what to measure instead, and how to have the metrics "birds and bees" conversation. | 7, 11 | Search Statistics Document (funnel) |
| You don't get all the information you need when a new requisition is opened so searches often stop and start and ultimately take too long | Of course, your hiring manager must make time for this discussion. It's easier when they see what's in it for them.<br><br>Then you can use this guide to ask all the essential questions about the position--the kinds of questions that can get the hiring manager to begin to see you as a consultant and business partner. | 5, 6 | Comprehensive launch document |
| There's no job description for the opening, the description is outdated and/or the hiring manager isn't entirely sure of the qualifications they are looking for. | It's not always easy for a hiring manager to craft a current job description. These questions will guide that process so you come out with a job description that helps ensure you and the hiring manager agree on what the right candidate looks like. | 6 | Comprehensive launch document |
| The hiring manager changes their mind about what they are looking for in the middle of a search | The position profile helps the hiring manager set out what they are looking for. When it seems like they are changing their mind, use the information from the launch meeting as the basis of a conversation to either can get the search back on track or figure out what the changes need to be—without damaging the partnership relationship. | 6, 13 | Strategy Sheet #3 |
| The Hiring manage does not understand the impact of today's economic climate on filling their open position. | These techniques will give you a clear idea of what the hiring manager wants, and non-confrontational ways to let that manager know what they are looking for may not exist or may be too expensive. They show you how to let the marketplace help the hiring manager understand what is possible in today's economy, whether it's robust or rotten. | 6, 9, 10, 13 | Comprehensive launch document |

| If your situation is… | Perspective | Use these tech-niques… | Use these tools… |
|---|---|---|---|
| Hiring manager is out of touch with the realities of the candidate marketplace today, including generational differences | Use questions to help your hiring manager tell you what they are really looking for, and then let the results in the marketplace help the hiring manager understand today's reality. | 6, 9, 10, 13 | Strategy Sheet #4 |
| Hiring managers do not feel they get to see enough quality candidates. | These techniques will help you and the hiring manager clearly define candidate quality. Plus you will see how to get feedback that is helpful. It may be that the candidate the hiring manager didn't like was exactly what they said they were looking for. | 6, 10 | Strategy Sheet #3 |
| Hiring Manager cannot seem to make a hiring decision without seeing lots more candidates. | There can be many reasons the hiring manager wants to see a lot of candidates, and the Position Profile facilitates a conversation to bring those reasons to light. | 8 | Comprehensive launch document |
| Hiring manager takes a long time deciding which candidates he/she wants to interview | After expectations about the timeline are set, commitments have been made that may not get met and/or there needs to be a non-confrontational discussion to get the timeline adjusted appropriately. These techniques will help you do those things. | 6, 8, 11 | Strategy Sheet #1 |
| The hiring manager does not give you feedback on resumes you've submitted or after interviews. | There are subtle easy ways to help the hiring manager give you feedback that is actually, well, feedback! Help them go beyond the words "not a fit." | 10 | Strategy Sheets #1 and 2 |
| Hiring manager keeps canceling or not showing up for interviews with candidates. | Sometimes different ways to elicit commitments can be very effective. It's also important to help a hiring manager understand the importance of the candidate experience—not just for the winning candidate but for all! | 7, 14 | Candidate Experience checklist |
| Hiring managers don't follow up on candidates who have interviewed. | Hiring managers often have not thought about the impact in the market place and on the success of the search that a poor candidate experience can create. This technique can put it in perspective for them. | 14 | Strategy Sheet #1 |
| Hiring managers drag their feet at decision time. | It's helpful to discuss with the hiring manager at the beginning of a search how many candidates they need to see before making a decision. If still no decisions, getting good feedback will help uncover what is preventing that decision. And it's important for everyone to understand the impact on candidates of a delay at this point. | 7, 10, 14 | Strategy Sheet #2 |

| If your situation is... | Perspective | Use these techniques... | Use these tools... |
|---|---|---|---|
| The company, or the compensation committee or the hiring manager don't want to pay a competitive salary and don't believe you when you tell them what it will take. | Nothing will speak as loudly as the data from the market. When you can show great candidates already at or above the compensation your company is offering, the decision makers now have data that supports making a change. If there isn't going to be a change, it's probably time for a discussion about what requirements can be loosened in order to find a candidate at the compensation range they are willing to pay. | 13 | Strategy Sheet #2 |

# Your Comprehensive Question Library

Sometimes it's helpful to have key groups of questions all in one place. So I created this list for you! While your relationship with the hiring manager is always the primary goal, these are arranged to help you create postings your ideal candidates cannot resist, plus be able to screen more quickly.

Some questions are in more than one group because I know you may only get to do one group of questions at a time. If that is your current environment, at least you will get everything you need in one particular area.

For this list, I wanted to help you accelerate the speed and increase quality/number of candidates first and then do the relationship building questions. So if you're feeling pressure to improve your recruiting statistics, this is the perfect order for you to start asking questions.

**Information helpful in gathering basics and the administrative details of the position**

- Title
- Location
- Compensation
- Is position new? If not, why is position open?
- Position reports to:
- What titles report to the position? How many of each?
- Responsibilities and job duties
- Experience and background of the ideal candidate (required, desired, helpful):
- Competencies (softer skills, e.g., leadership, team player, self-motivated, etc.):
- Is any telecommuting possible in this position?
- Required travel %, locations, % overnight/weekly, reasons
- Is there a relocation package for this position?
- If not, would you consider candidates from outside the area if they relocate themselves?

**Information to help create a more marketing-focused job description and posting (and any emails or other communications directly to targeted candidates)**

- What makes this a great career opportunity?
- What does this opportunity offer that will be exciting to the candidates?
- What is happening in the company overall, this portion of the company, etc., that would be important for the candidate to know?
- What does the near term future look like? What new things are you planning?
- What are you excited about in your business?
- How would you describe the culture today? What is it like to work in this group?
- Is any telecommuting possible in this position?
- Required travel %
- Is there a relocation package for this position?
- If not, would you consider candidates from outside the area if they relocate themselves?

**Questions that can help you with sourcing strategy.**

- If you have done a similar search, what were the challenges?
- What did you learn about the marketplace?
- What was successful that you would like to have done again?
- What didn't work?
- What have you done so far on the search? Postings? Interviews? (Would like names of people considered regardless of outcome.)
- What has been done to generate employee referrals?
- Are there any of your LinkedIn connections we should contact?
- Would you be willing to add a status update to your LinkedIn profile that you are hiring for this position?
- Target Companies (competitions, parallel industries, end users):
- Most important sources for this position:
- Companies not of interest (because of their culture, business practices, etc., that would make employees incompatible with us):
- Companies off limits (where there may be partnership agreements, joint ventures, etc., that would be jeopardized if we hired someone away from them):

**Ask these questions of your hiring manager so you can get the candidates engaged and excited**

- Is this a new position or a replacement?
- Is there a team reporting to this position? How many? Titles?
- Will there be a need to increase the team over time?
- Is the team fully function or are there items for the incoming manager to address (training, replacement, morale issues, etc.)?
- Job objectives to be achieved within first 6 months. Which is the most important; what makes it the most important?
- How does this position fit into the long-term strategic goals for the organization?
- Career growth potential (either promotionally, acquiring new skills, etc.)
- What makes this a great career opportunity?
- What is happening in the company overall, this portion of the company, etc., that would be important for the candidate to know?
- What does the near term future look like? What new things are you planning?
- What are you excited about in your business?
- How would you describe the culture today? What is it like to work in this group?
- What is you like to work for? What is your personal style, preferred management style, etc.?
- For relatively new managers, what specifically made you join the company?
- What are you most enjoying about the company and your role?

**Questions that will add to your understanding of the role and what the hiring manager is really looking for**

- Success factors of predecessor or the best people in the position. What do/did they do that is different than average? If there was someone in the position just recently, ask: What did that person do that you would like to see the person we hire also do?
- Job objectives to be achieved within first 6 months. Which is the most important; what makes it the most important?
- What is the most important task for this position? What makes it important to you?
- What are the key issues this person would need to address short-term? Longer-term? Internal and external?
- Any challenges to success? Internal? External?

- 3 –5 key questions you would like us to ask candidates as a part of our screening process? (Be sure to ask them how to identify a good answer.)

1.

2.

3.

- Are there key categories of people you are looking for (e.g., hard charger, creative, intellectually curious, etc.)?
- If so, how do you define those terms?
- How do you know when you're sitting across from a great candidate?

## Information to help identify candidates meeting the hiring manager's requirements

- Background/qualifications of predecessor
- Success factors of predecessor or the best people in the position. What do/did they do that is different than average? If there was someone in the position just recently, ask: What did that person do that you would like to see the person we hire also do?
- Job objectives to be achieved within first 6 months. Which is the most important; what makes it the most important?
- What is the most important task for this position? What makes it important to you?
- What are the key issues this person would need to address short-term? Longer-term? Internal and external?
- Experience and background of the ideal candidate (required, desired, helpful):
- Competencies (softer skills, e.g., leadership, team player, self-motivated, etc.):
- Any challenges to success? Internal? External?
- Are there 3 –5 key questions you would like us to ask candidates as a part of our screening process? (Be sure to ask them how to identify a good answer.)

1.

2.

3.

- Are there key categories of people you are looking for (e.g., hard charger, creative, intellectually curious, etc.)?
- If so, how do you define those terms?
- How do you know when you're sitting across from a great candidate?

## Information to help get more timely information and/or participation by the hiring manager

- How does the hiring manager want to receive resumes for review, e.g., one at a time via email, once a week in a phone call or meeting with you, when you have a certain number ready for review, etc.?
- If the hiring manager has been slow getting you the necessary feedback in the past, ask what would make that step easier for them.
- How soon, on average, will the hiring manager get back to you on resumes?
- Initially ask how soon they can let you know their thoughts on resumes or candidates.
- Let them pick a length of time that works for them.
- Hiring Manager's definition of success for this search:

- Hiring Manager's definition of quality service from the recruiter:
- Recruiting team's definition of quality support from the Hiring Manager:
- Hiring Manager's expectations regarding time to fill:
- Discussion of timing requirements that may present a challenge:
- Discussion of other items that may be a challenge in this search:

**Questions that will help you get to know the hiring manager as well as continue to build your relationship**

- What does the near term future look like? What new things are you planning?
- What are you excited about in your business?
- What is you like to work for? What is your personal style, preferred management style, etc.?
- For relatively new managers, what specifically made you join the company?
- What are you most enjoying about the company and your role?
- For relatively new managers, what specifically made you join the company?
- What are you most enjoying about the company and your role?

**Questions to help with any challenges in the interview process (especially important if your hiring manager seems to want everyone but the night cleaning crew to be involved in the interview schedule)**

- What will be the first step in the process? Will you want us to meet the candidate before you meet them?
- If you like the candidate, what are the next steps? Who interviews at each step? If anyone cannot be scheduled on a timely basis, can we skip them or are they a required interview?
- If the first candidate meets your requirements and seems to have the skills and personality to do the job, would you be willing to move them to offer?
- If not, how many candidates do you feel you would like to see in order to feel comfortable with your hiring decision?
- Does everyone in the interview process agree on what this position will do and the requirements?
- Do you want some people to interview for specific skills/experiences? Do they know what their role is?
- Who gets to have a vote on hiring the candidate and who just gets to have input. Does everyone understand that distinction?
- What is the biggest benefit you get as the hiring manager from having this interview process you've laid out?
- How to you want to gather information from all the interviewees to help you make your hiring decision?
- Will you want to try to have all candidates to interview on the same day? How will that day be structured?
- If holding candidates already in process to find sufficient number of candidates to form a slate is not feasible, are you flexible on moving people through the process rather than hold everyone until a slate is created?
- How long does the typical process take from first interview to offer decision?
- How many candidates do you typically want to see at first interview stage?
- How many candidates do you typically move to 2nd and beyond interviews before choosing a finalist and making an offer?
- Are things like preparing a 90-day business plan, giving a presentation, etc., part of your process?
- The recruiter will contact the candidate within a couple of hours to gather feedback after each interview. Would you like that feedback via phone or email?
- How soon after you hear the candidate feedback will you get you feedback and next steps for the candidate, if any, to us?

**Referencing Process**

- If there is an established referencing process in your organization, the following may not be necessary.
- Do you typically want referencing conducted in addition to that done as part of your offer process?

- If yes, at what point in the process?
- What references do you want the candidate to furnish, and how many of each?
- Will you want us to conduct the referencing?
- Will you furnish us additional areas to be probed during the referencing?
- Do you want the results verbally or in a summary report? (Neither format will attribute comments to a particular reference.)
- Do you typically talk to any of the references either in our place or after we have talked to them?
- Do you typically try to find people not supplied by the candidate to serve as references?

## Compensation and Offer

- At what point in the interview process do you typically have compensation discussions with candidates?
- What do those discussions include?
- At what point in the process will you expect the recruiter to have a clear understanding of what compensation (base, bonus, stock, etc.) the candidate might be looking for?
- When you are at that point, will you discuss the possible offer with the recruiter or would you just like the info the recruiter has via email?
- Who will make the offer to the candidate?

# Recruiting Satisfaction Survey  Sample

Please take a few minutes to respond to the below questionnaire. The feedback you provide is instrumental in helping us identify what is working well and where improvements must be made within the staffing model.

Please respond to the following questions regarding your recent experience hiring a new employee into your department. Please feel free to add any comments in the section below.

**1)Strongly Disagree 2)Disagree 3)Neither agree or disagree 4) Agree 5)Strongly Agree**

1.  The recruiter consulted with me and set clear expectations on the staffing process steps and timing.

Rating _____

2.  The recruiter sought to understand the job requirements and needs of my business.

Rating _____

3.  The recruiter provided me with an adequate number of sourcing options to identify candidates, including cost and timing implications.

Rating _____

4.  The recruiter was knowledgeable on the current market conditions and consulted with me to insure my needs and requirements were in line with the market.

Rating _____

5.  The recruiter presented qualified candidates to me within the agreed upon timeframe.

Rating _____

6.  The candidates presented to me were appropriate and screened to my minimal specifications.

Rating _____

7.  I received prompt and continual feedback throughout the process from the recruiter.

Rating _____

8.  The recruiter was responsive and quickly able to resolve any issues that arose.

Rating _____

9. Overall, the time to fill my position met my expectations was reasonable and aligned with what was agreed upon with the recruiter.

Rating _____

10. Overall, I am satisfied with the quality of service that I received from the recruiter.

Rating _____

Please include any additional comments or suggestions about the service you received, the staffing process or the staffing team:

_____

_____

# Delivering Bad News Worksheet

| STEPS | NOTES, OBSERVATONS, CHALLENGES, RESULTS, ETC. |
|---|---|
| **Here's where we are:**<br><br>Explain current situation. Take responsibility for your part but not for those things beyond your control.<br><br>Share your thought process & identify issues. Briefly explain what your observation/concern is—what's really causing this issue? | |
| **Here's what we are both trying to accomplish:**<br><br>Build a bridge: point out areas of agreement. Focus on the issues and desired results non-emotionally. Express desire to constructively come to a go-forward plan that both of you agree upon.<br><br>Ask a transitional question, e.g., "Where do you think we should go from here?" or "This is what I'm thinking might work. What do you think?" | |
| **Here's what we could change:**<br><br>Mutually agree on next steps: Brainstorm ideas. Remember that this is an issue for the two of you to solve. Ask for ideas from the hiring manager.<br><br>Should the desired results be changed? The assumptions? The process?<br><br>At the same time, you're the recruiting consultant, so be prepared to evaluate suggestions when the brainstorming is over. | |
| **Here's what we will do:**<br><br>Be sure the hiring manager agrees to all areas being changed. If you need the hiring manager to do something, e.g., check with the compensation group to get the salary raised, be sure to get the commitment to do that and an expected date of completion.<br><br>Make your commitments clear as to what you will do, and the timeframe in which you will see the results. | |

| | |
|---|---|
| **Here is how we'll follow up:**<br><br>Suggest follow-up discussion to evaluate the results from the new agreements you and the hiring manager have made. Be specific about when/where/how that discussion will take place. | |

# Candidate Experience Best Practices

| Best Practice | Current | Opportunity to Enhance |
|---|---|---|
| Treat applicants in alignment with your values and brand. Keep them informed on a regular and frequent basis of their status, next steps, the anticipated time line, etc. | | |
| There are substantive differences between passive and active candidates in terms of the impact and importance of the candidate experience. Passive candidates may need more: "romancing," time to schedule interviews, etc. | | |
| Respect an applicant's time when you request information from them. | | |
| Make sure all applicants go through the same process, get asked the same questions, have to meet the same expectations, etc. | | |
| 1st contact should be structured to create and/or heighten candidate's interest and set expectations for the process, as well as gather basic information to insure the candidate is viable based on experience, salary, etc., on a high level. | | |
| Give information beyond the job description to the candidate early in the process. Give the candidate insight into what it's like to work for your company, what the people are like there, etc. | | |
| Limit the number of interviews to a reasonable number, so that the applicant does not suffer through an interview gauntlet. Research findings show that excessive interviews add little to selection accuracy and usually serve only to slow the hiring process and frustrate applicants, especially those who are currently employed. | | |
| Respect the applicant's current boss and job-related time constraints by making a good-faith effort to provide interview times and locations that fit the applicant's needs. | | |
| Use interview process to give candidates additional info about the job, culture, etc. It should not be all about the assessment/evaluation of the candidate. | | |
| Coordinate questions among all interviewers so the candidate does not get the same set of questions from every person they meet. | | |

| | | |
|---|---|---|
| Provide the candidate feedback on how they are seen as a fit for the opportunity as soon as possible after the interviews, as well as solicit their feedback on how they feel about the opportunity, process, and people they are meeting, etc. | | |
| Provide an experience such that candidates are excited and energized by the possibility of working for the company. If they are not going to be moving forward in the process, "next steps" should not be discussed. If there is interest in the candidate, they should know that when they leave. You can lose desirable candidates if they leave the interview without feeling you are interested in them. | | |

# Recruiting Funnel

| DATES |
|---|
| |
| |
| |
| |
| |
| |
| |
| |
| Notes: |

Totals: LI Profiles Reviewed & Resumes Received, etc.

Potential Candidates Reviewed

Candidates Screened by Recruiter

Candidates Presented to Hiring Manager

Hiring Manager Interviews

Offers Made

Hires

| TOTALS |
|---|
| |
| |
| |
| |
| |
| |
| |
| |
| Notes: |

# Consultative Recruiting Forms, Templates & Reports

You can have all the forms mentioned in this guide in word document format by going to the link below.

You will get:

- Comprehensive Search Launch Document,
- Delivering Bad News Worksheet,
- Recruiting Satisfaction Survey,
- Recruiting Funnel Diagram,
- Candidate Experience Best Practices,

Please feel free to modify them to fit your situations, each of your hiring managers, each position you are recruiting for, etc.

There are also copies of the special reports available in case you would like to print them out and have them handy.

Please download all the forms, templates and reports by going to:

https://TheConsultativeRecruiter.com/bonuses

**For more resources, or to talk about training and coaching, please give me a call:**
**832.464.4447**
**Or schedule a call here:**
https://meetme.so/AllAboutYou

# Now It's Your Turn

I'm really excited for you because I've seen how these techniques have given recruiters back their confidence, made recruiting fun again, and built strong relationships with their hiring managers.

If you ever have questions or situations you would like to brainstorm with me, don't hesitate to call on me!

I know we would be able to come up with great new perspectives.

Best wishes for:

- More qualified candidates
- Faster times to fill, and most importantly,
- Happier hiring managers

Warm regards,

katherine@ConsultativeRecruiting.com
832.464.4447
https://meetme.so/AllAboutYou

Please download all the forms, templates and reports by going to:

https://TheConsultativeRecruiter.com/bonuses